Prepared in cooperation with the University of Arizona

Use of Normalized Difference Vegetation Index (NDVI) Habitat Models to Predict Breeding Birds on the San Pedro River, Arizona

Open-File Report 2013–1100

U.S. Department of the Interior
U.S. Geological Survey

U.S. Department of the Interior
SALLY JEWELL, Secretary

U.S. Geological Survey
Suzette M. Kimball, Acting Director

U.S. Geological Survey, Reston, Virginia: 2013

For more information on the USGS—the Federal source for science about the Earth,
its natural and living resources, natural hazards, and the environment—visit
http://www.usgs.gov or call 1–888–ASK–USGS

For an overview of USGS information products, including maps, imagery, and publications,
visit *http://www.usgs.gov/pubprod*

Suggested citation:
McFarland, T. M. and van Riper, Charles III, 2013, Use of Normalized Difference Vegetation Index (NDVI) habitat
models to predict breeding birds on the San Pedro River, Arizona: U.S. Geological Survey Open-File Report
2013–1100. 42 p.

Any use of trade, product, or firm names is for descriptive purposes only and does not imply
endorsement by the U.S. Government.

Contents

Use of Normalized Difference Vegetation Index (NDVI) Habitat Modeling to Predict Breeding Birds on the San Pedro River, Arizona

By Tiffany Marie McFarland and Charles van Riper III

Abstract

Successful management practices of avian populations depend on understanding relationships between birds and their habitat, especially in rare habitats, such as riparian areas of the desert Southwest. Remote-sensing technology has become popular in habitat modeling, but most of these models focus on single species, leaving their applicability to understanding broader community structure and function largely untested. We investigated the usefulness of two Normalized Difference Vegetation Index (NDVI) habitat models to model avian abundance and species richness on the upper San Pedro River in southeastern Arizona. Although NDVI was positively correlated with our bird metrics, the amount of explained variation was low. We then investigated the addition of vegetation metrics and other remote-sensing metrics to improve our models. Although both vegetation metrics and remotely sensed metrics increased the power of our models, the overall explained variation was still low, suggesting that general avian community structure may be too complex for NDVI models.

Chapter 1: Introduction

Why Investigate Multi-Species Remote-Sensing Models in Desert Riparian Habitats?

Successful management practices depend on understanding how populations of animals are distributed within their environment and specifically the relationships between animals and their habitat (Kantrud and Stewart, 1984; Wiens and Rotenberry, 1985; Debinski and Brussard, 1994; Colwell and Dodd, 1995). A key first step in conservation and management is to understand the availability, distribution, and use of habitat. Understanding these relationships is especially important to the conservation and management of species that are dependent on habitats in ecosystems that are rare or threatened by degradation, such as riparian areas of the U.S. desert Southwest. Riparian woodlands, predominantly of Fremont cottonwood (*Populus fremontii*) and Goodding's willow (*Salix gooddingii*), constitute a small percentage of the landscape, yet support a high diversity and high density of avian species (Knopf and others, 1988). These riparian systems form ribbons of green vegetation in the otherwise dry landscape and are used by birds as migratory stopover sites (Skagen and others, 1998; Yong and Finch, 2002; DeLong and others, 2005) and as breeding habitat for many species (Strong and Bock, 1990; DeSante and George, 1994), providing water, shade, food, and cover from predators. However, riparian areas have been degraded because of stresses from agriculture, overgrazing, altered hydrologic regimes, and the invasion of ornamental plants from the genus *Tamarix*, called "salt cedar"

(*Tamarix* spp.) or "tamarisk," beginning in the late 1800s (Robinson, 1965; Knopf and others, 1988; Earnst and others, 2005; Stromberg and others, 2007). Tamarisk had been notoriously credited to many negative ecological and economic effects (Cleverly and others, 1997; Shafroth and others, 2005) because the plant can establish itself in dry, salty conditions when cottonwood and willow cannot (Glenn and Nagler, 2005). When a river system is already subject to other stresses, such as altered streamflow or high salinity, monotypic stands of tamarisk can form (Shafroth and others, 2002). Much debate exists over what the management strategy of tamarisk should be (Shafroth and others, 2005), but the plant generally has been viewed as unsuitable habitat for breeding birds (Hunter and others, 1988; Ellis, 1995). However, new scientific evidence casts doubt on this view (Yard and others, 2004; Paxton and others, 2007; Durst and others, 2008; Sogge and others, 2008; van Riper and others, 2008;).

Damage to southwestern riparian systems already has been linked to decreases in populations of many avian species that rely on riparian habitat for any or all parts of the year (Knopf and others, 1988; DeSante and George, 1994). For instance, the southwestern Willow Flycatcher (SWWF; *Empidonax traillii extimus*) winters in tropical forests in Central America and comes north to the rivers and washes of the Desert Southwest only to breed (Sedgwick, 2000), but without adequate breeding grounds, the species is in decline (DeSante and George, 1994; Hatten and Paradzick, 2003). Many other species that use these rivers during the breeding season also are showing signs of decline, including Bell's vireo (BEVI; *Vireo bellii*), Lucy's warbler (LUWA; *Vermivora luciae*), and Abert's towhee (ABTO; *Pipilo aberti*) (Rea, 1983; Knopf and others, 1988; DeSante and George, 1994), all of which were listed on the Arizona Audubon Watch List (http://az.audubon.org/arizona-watchlist-2007).

In avian ecology, however, traditional methods of monitoring birds are costly in terms of money and time. Monitoring birds requires long hours in the field, yet avian activity patterns allow censuses to take place mostly in the early morning (Robbins, 1981). Additionally, because of property rights or remote field locations, access and logistics can be difficult.

In 1972, satellite imagery became widely available to the public, and since then researchers have been investigating the use of such data in monitoring avian populations (Gottschalk and others, 2005). However, these models are largely designed to describe the habitat of a single species, and the usefulness of remote sensing to describe habitat of avian communities more generally has gone largely untested (Gottschalk and others, 2005). Many of these models use remotely sensed characteristics of the physical landscape that may have bearing beyond just the species for which the model is designed and, therefore, may be applicable to the status and management strategies of multiple species.

About Remote Sensing and Normalized Difference Vegetation NDVI Models

Geographic Information Systems (GIS) and remote-sensing technology and algorithms allow monitoring of changes to the Earth's surface on larger spatial and temporal scales than are feasible through ground census techniques. Remotely sensed data are an interpretation of various spectral signals that reach a sensor after interacting with objects on the Earth's surface, and these interpretations can reveal many physical characteristics of that object, including surface elevation, temperature, and various aspects of the vegetation and land cover (Melesse and others, 2007). Combined with spatial mapping using GIS tools, these remotely sensed elements of the natural environment (for example, vegetation, topography, and proximity to human developments or other physical features) can be used to define and model suitable habitat for different species (Guisan and Zimmerman, 2000; Gottschalk and others, 2005). Models like these have become widely used to identify, characterize, monitor, and predict the range, breeding sites, or response to land-management strategies of many avian species (Palmeirim, 1988; Tucker and others, 1997; Gibson and others, 2004; Newbold and Eadie, 2004; Mathieu and others, 2006). Gottschalk and others (2005) summarized 109 studies over three decades that used remote sensing to model avian habitat, but the techniques also have been applied to habitats of many other types of organisms (Mladdenoff and others, 1995; Hansen and others, 2001; Coops and Catling, 2002; Danks and Klein, 2002; Luoto and others, 2002; Greaves and others, 2006).

Metrics that use spectral reflectance pertinent to plants are called vegetation indices (VI), the most popular of which is NDVI. NDVI is sensitive to active photosynthetic compounds and is therefore a popular way to measure the productivity of vegetation, or "greenness," in a defined area (Tucker, 1979; Tucker and others, 1985). This VI is one of many spectral ratios, but is simple in that it uses the percent reflectance of two bands of the electromagnetic spectrum: the visible red (R; 0.4–0.7 μm) and the near-infrared (NIR; 0.7–1.1 μm), which is related to the green biomass of a plant (Nixon and others, 1985) because it is a ratio of NIR energy scattered to visible light energy absorbed in the red wavelength (Jordan, 1969). NDVI is calculated by dividing the difference between these spectral bands by their sum, yielding a value between -1 and 1 (Tucker and others, 1985):

NDVI=(NIR-R) / (NIR+R)   [eq. 1]

Because NDVI is a spectral measurement of the photosynthesis occurring in a defined spatial area, the value generally increases throughout the growing season, and then decreases during the plants' senescent period. Additionally, NDVI can change from year to year because of environmental changes, like amount of rainfall or temperatures in the prior seasons (Prasad and others, 2008). Therefore, researchers must be careful to ensure the NDVI imagery being used corresponds to the timeframe of other correlated data.

Because NDVI is a measurement of an area's primary productivity, we would expect this metric to relate to the abundances of organisms the area can support. For example, Mills and others (1991) determined that total vegetation density was highly correlated with breeding bird density in southwestern shrub and desert habitat, and similarly, abundance has been shown to increase with NDVI (Maurer, 1994; Osborne and others, 2001). NDVI also has been shown to correlate with avian species richness (Lee and others, 2004). Seto and others (2004) showed that the maximum NDVI value within a satellite pixel of Landsat Thematic Mapper™ imagery (30-m^2 resolution) within two different landscape scales (segments of canyons and entire canyons) correlates with bird species richness (also Bailey and others, 2004). NDVI also has been shown to correlate with avian species richness when applied to very coarse imagery (250-m^2 resolution) if location is a covariate (Foody, 2005). However, most of these models take into account NDVI over large continuous tracts of habitat, and the application of remote-sensing models to long, narrow habitats such as riparian systems is rare.

One such model, a species-specific habitat model that uses NDVI, was developed in 1999 for the riparian zones along the San Pedro and Gila Rivers of southern Arizona. The SWWF model developed by the Arizona Game and Fish Department successfully predicts breeding sites of this endangered subspecies of the Willow Flycatcher (Hatten and Paradzick, 2003). The SWWF model uses a logistic regression equation to assign a probability of the occurrence of a SWWF nest to each 30-m^2 pixel of Landsat™ imagery based on a combination of statistics derived from NDVI and the size of the floodplain obtained from a digital elevation model (DEM). Probability for the SWWF model is calculated as (Hatten and Sogge, 2007):

Probability = exp(logit)/1+exp(logit), where the logit is
1.483(NDVI)+0.098(NDVIBEST)+0.034(FLOODPL)+0.648(NDVISTD)–6.074
where,
NDVI = dense vegetation (NDVI>0.33) at the site (0.09 ha, 30 m^2)
NDVIBEST = amount (%) of densest vegetation (NDVI>0.41) within a 4.5-ha (120-m radius) neighborhood

FLOODPL = amount (%) of floodplain or flat terrain (<2.5 degrees) within a 41-ha (approximately 360 m radius) neighborhood

DVISTD = Standard Deviation (SD) in NDVI (12 classes) within a 4.5-ha (120-m radius) neighborhood

This probability was then used to separate the riparian vegetation into five probability classes: Class 1 = 1-20 percent, Class 2 = 21–40 percent, Class 3 = 41–60 percent, Class 4 = 61–80 percent, and Class 5 = 81–98 percent probability. The SWWF model successfully predicted riparian areas with the highest SWWF nest densities along the San Pedro and Gila Rivers (Hatten and Paradzick, 2003) and was equally successful when implemented on the Rio Grande River in New Mexico (Hatten and Sogge, 2007). The SWWF model also was applied to the entire State of Arizona using 2001 imagery to delineate all regions of suitable breeding habitat for SWWF in the State (Dockens and others, 2004).

Because vegetation and floodplain size are landscape characteristics that are potentially important to all riparian bird species (Strong and Bock, 1990), this model may be applicable to the management of other species of breeding birds in the riparian areas of the desert Southwest.

Objectives

We investigated the usefulness of the SWWF model in modeling avian species richness, abundance, and community structure by investigating whether (1) the five probability classes (Classes 0–5) as defined by the SWWF model, (2) the probability value (P) as a continuous variable, and (3) a simpler model, the NDVI value alone; relate to several defined species of concern, the abundance of birds, and species richness. Probability is the continuous variable representing the probability of a SWWF nest being present at each location (0–0.98), while the probability Classes represent the continuous probability value split into increments of 0.2 (20 percent probability).

We then further investigated the relationships between NDVI, birds, and vegetation, and determined whether the addition of vegetation metrics and other metrics derived from satellite imagery could improve the use of NDVI for modeling general avian community structure on the San Pedro River in southeastern Arizona.

In order to find additional metrics for modeling avian distributions, we first investigated what vegetation parameters best predict NDVI. We wanted to determine if approximate NDVI values can be assessed by observing the vegetation present on a site. Land managers could then assess remotely sensed metrics without need of satellite imagery.

Secondly, we wanted to determine what vegetation parameters best predict birds. If vegetation parameters could be used to predict bird richness or abundance, satellite imagery may not be necessary to assess avian habitat.

Thirdly, we wanted to determine if vegetation parameters added to NDVI are a better model for use in predicting bird abundance and species richness than NDVI alone, and to understand whether the addition of vegetation parameters increases the strength of NDVI.

And finally, we wanted to determine whether other metrics derived from NDVI can be used to strengthen the capacity of NDVI to predict bird presence, and whether this type of model is stronger than those including vegetation parameters. If other remotely sensed metrics can be used in place of vegetation data, on-the-ground vegetation surveys would not be necessary. The only necessary on-the-ground work would be to verify the model output, thus reducing the time and resources involved in monitoring avian habitat. This would increase the efficiency of surveys for conservation and management strategies.

Structure of the Following Chapters

An overview of our study and summary of our most important findings are presented in Chapter 2. The expanse of our research is reported within two following appendixes, A and B. Tables and figures referenced in each appendix appear at the end of each respective appendix. Each appendix has an individual literature citation section. The methods, results, and conclusions of this study are contained in each appendix.

Chapter 2: Present Study

Abstract of Appendix A: Extension of Riparian NDVI Models to Avian Abundance and Richness

Understanding community-habitat relationships is important for the conservation of avian species in the disappearing riparian areas of the Southwestern United States, but monitoring avian populations can be difficult and expensive. Although remote-sensing technology has become popular in habitat modeling, satellite imagery habitat models focus on single species, and the applicability of these models to understanding broader community structure and function remains largely untested. In this analysis, we assess the applicability of using a Normalized Difference Vegetation Index (NDVI) Southwestern Willow Flycatcher habitat model (SWWF model), as well as a simple NDVI model, to predict breeding bird abundance and species richness in riparian areas of southern Arizona. Using avian point counts, vegetation surveys, and remote-sensing data from three breeding seasons, we determined that the SWWF model weakly correlates with avian community abundance, species richness, or avian species of conservation concern. However, NDVI, the SWWF model main component, showed a strong relationship, even when averaged over large spatial scales, suggesting that NDVI alone is a suitable metric for monitoring bird communities. The acquisition of global NDVI imagery is free and simple to obtain, making NDVI a potentially valuable tool for land managers.

Abstract of Appendix B: Comparison of NDVI Models for Riparian Avian Abundance and Species Richness

Understanding the relationships between avian species and their habitat and identifying habitat availability is a key component in the development of successful management practices. Remote-sensing models could make monitoring avian communities and their habitat more cost effective and timely than traditional methods, but the applicability of these models to understanding broader community structure and function remains largely untested. A remote-sensing metric, Normalized Difference Vegetation Index (NDVI), has been shown to be positively correlated with avian abundance and species richness (McFarland and others, 2012; Maurer, 1994; Lee and others, 2004). In this analysis, we investigate the use of two types of additional metrics, vegetation metrics measured on the ground and remote-sensing metrics derived from satellite imagery, to strengthen our NDVI models. Although adding remotely sensed metrics to NDVI did increase the amount of variation explained, models including vegetation tended to best predict bird abundance and avian species richness, with or without NDVI. However, the amount of variation shown by even the best models is still low, indicating that NDVI habitat models may not work as well for avian communities as they do for individual species.

Summary of Findings

The broad scope of this study was to examine the use of remote sensing in modeling avian abundance and avian species richness along desert riparian areas of Arizona. The remote-sensing habitat models and analyses reported in this study appreciably advance our understanding of the application of these models, especially to bird communities. Study results are summarized below, organized by the appendix in which they are detailed.

From Appendix A: Extension of Riparian NDVI Models to Avian Abundance and Richness

NDVI had a positive linear relationship with species richness and bird abundance, and explained more variation than Probability in both models. This positive relationship with bird abundance and species richness was sustained even when the NDVI values were averaged over large areas, simulating coarse-resolution imagery. As the pixel size became larger, the amount of explained variability (R^2) was reduced, but the relationship still existed. In all of our models, bird abundance had less unexplained variation than richness when modeled by NDVI.

From Appendix B: Comparison of NDVI Models for Riparian Avian Abundance and Species Richness

We determined that the addition of vegetation parameters and other remotely sensed parameters to NDVI increased the amount of variation that is explained in our models; that the best models to predict avian abundance include NDVI with either remote-sensing or vegetation metrics; and that the best models to predict species richness include vegetation metrics, with or without NDVI. However, the increases in explained variation are small and a large amount of variation still remains unexplained.

Certain patterns were consistent in our models. We can conclude that in general, species richness and abundance increase with an increase in NDVI and an increase in total cover. The presence of water also increased avian abundance. Our data also show that more birds and more species exist in areas where the riparian area is wide and in areas with more canopy cover and more cottonwoods, reinforcing the importance of conserving and reestablishing cottonwood and willow gallery forests along rivers (Brand and others, 2008).

In summary, our data indicate that NDVI models may not be as successful at modeling general avian community structure as opposed to individual species. Because vegetation structure is so important in modeling bird assemblages, future investigations should examine how these particular vegetation parameters can be gathered more easily by remote-sensing techniques, either using vegetation indices or aerial photography. Additionally, the use of purely remote-sensed metrics should be further investigated for species of conservation concern in riparian areas of the desert Southwest to ensure the future monitoring and management of these at-risk species.

References Cited

Bailey, S.A., Horner-Devine, M.C., Luck, G., Moore, L.A., Carney, K.M., Anderson, S., Betrus, C., and Fleishman, E., 2004, Primary productivity and species richness—Relationships among functional guilds, residency groups and vagility classes at multiple spatial scales: Ecography, v. 27, p. 207–217.

Brand, L.A., White, G.C., and Noon, B.R., 2008, Factors influencing species richness and community composition of breeding birds in a desert riparian corridor: The Condor, v. 110, p. 199–210.

Cleverly, J.R., Smith, S.D., Sala, A., and Devitt, D.A., 1997, Invasive capacity of *Tamarix ramosissima* in a Mojave Desert floodplain—The role of drought: Oecologia, v. 111, p. 12–18.

Colwell, M.A., and Dodd, S.L., 1995, Waterbird communities and habitat relationships in coastal pastures of northern California: Conservation Biology, v. 9, p. 827–834.

Coops, N.C., and Catling, P.C., 2002, Prediction of the spatial distribution and relative abundance of ground-dwelling mammals using remote sensing imagery and simulation models: Landscape Ecology, v. 17, p. 173–188.

Danks, F.S., and Klein, D.R., 2002, Using GIS to predict potential wildlife habitat: a case study of muskoxen in northern Alaska: International Journal of Remote Sensing, v. 23, p. 4611–4632.

Debinski, D.M., and Brussard, P.F., 1994, Using biodiversity data to assess species-habitat relationships in Glacier National Park, Montana: Ecological Applications, v. 4, p. 833–843.

De Long, J.P., Cox, S.W., and Cox, N.S., 2005, A comparison of avian use of high- and low-elevation sites during autumn migration in central New Mexico: Journal of Field Ornithology, v. 76, p. 326–333.

DeSante, D.F., and George, T.L., 1994, Population trends in the landbirds of western North America: Studies in Avian Biology, v. 15, p. 173–190.

Dockens, P.E.T., Paradzick, C.E., and Hatten, J.R., 2004, Application of a southwestern willow flycatcher GIS-based habitat model—An estimate of breeding habitat in Arizona, 2001, *in* Dockens, P.E.T., and Paradzick, C.E., eds., Mapping and monitoring southwestern willow flycatcher breeding habitat in Arizona—A remote sensing approach: Nongame and Endangered Wildlife Program Technical Report 223, Arizona Game and Fish Department, Phoenix, p. 28–59.

Durst, S.L., Theimer, T.C., Paxton, E.H., and Sogge, M.K., 2008, Temporal variation in the arthropod community of desert riparian habitats with varying amounts of saltcedar (*Tamarix ramosissima*): Journal of Arid Environments, v. 72, p. 1644–1653.

Earnst, S.L., Ballard, J.A., and Dobkin, D.S., 2005, Riparian songbird abundance a decade after cattle removal on Hart Mountain and Sheldon National Wildlife Refuges: USDA Forest Service General Technical Report PSW-GTR-191, Washington, D.C.

Ellis, L.M., 1995, Bird use of saltcedar and cottonwood vegetation in the Middle Rio Grande Valley of New Mexico, U.S.A.: Journal of Arid Environments, v. 30, p. 339–349.

Foody, G.M., 2005, Mapping the richness and composition of British breeding birds from coarse spatial resolution satellite sensor imagery: International Journal of Remote Sensing, v. 26, p. 3943–3956.

Gibson, L.A., Wilson, B.A., Cahill, D.M., and Hill, J., 2004, Spatial prediction of rufous bristlebird habitat in a coastal heathland—A GIS-based approach: Journal of Applied Ecology, v. 41, p. 213–223.

Glenn, E.P., and Nagler, P.L., 2005, Comparative ecophysiology of *Tamarix ramosissima* and native trees in western U.S. riparian zones: Journal of Arid Environments, v. 61, p. 419–446.

Gottschalk, T.K., Huettmann, F., and Ehlers, M., 2005, Thirty years of analysing and modeling avian habitat relationships using satellite imagery data: a review: International Journal of Remote Sensing, v. 26, p. 2631–2656.

Greaves, G.J., Mathieu, R., and Seddon, P.J., 2006, Predictive modeling and ground validation of the spatial distribution of the New Zealand long-tailed bat (*Chalinolobus tuberculatus*): Biological Conservation, v. 132, p. 211–221.

Guisan, A., and Zimmerman, N.E., 2000, Predictive habitat distribution models in ecology: Ecological Modelling, v. 135, p. 147–186.

Hansen, M.J., Franklin, S.E., Woudsma, C.G., and Peterson, M., 2001, Caribou habitat mapping and fragmentation analysis using Landsat MSS, TM, and GIS data in the North Columbia Mountains, British Columbia, Canada: Remote Sensing of Environment, v. 77, p. 50–65.

Hatten, J.R., and Paradzick, C.E., 2003, A multiscaled model of Southwestern Willow Flycatcher breeding habitat: The Journal of Wildlife Management, v. 67, p. 774–788.

Hatten, J.R., and Sogge, M.K., 2007, Using a remote sensing/GIS model to predict southwestern Willow Flycatcher breeding habitat along the Rio Grande, New Mexico: U.S. Geological Survey Open-File Report 2007–1207. (Also available at *http://pubs.usgs.gov/of/2007/1207/*.)

Hunter, W.C., Ohmart, R.D., and Anderson, B.W., 1988, Use of exotic saltcedar (*Tamarix chinensis*) by birds in arid riparian systems: The Condor, v. 90, p. 113–123.

Jordan, C.F., 1969, Derivation of leaf-area index from quality of light on the forest floor: Ecology, v. 50, p. 663–666.

Kantrud, H.A., and Stewart, R.E., 1984, Ecological distribution and crude density of breeding birds on prairie wetlands: The Journal of Wildlife Management, v. 48, p. 426–437.

Knopf, F.L., Johnson, R.R., Rich, T., Samson, F.B., and Szaro, R.C., 1988, Conservation of riparian ecosystems in the United States: Wilson Bulletin, v. 100, p. 272–284.

Lee, P., Ding, T., Hsu, F., and Geng, S., 2004, Breeding bird species richness in Taiwan: distribution on gradients of elevation, primary productivity and urbanization: Journal of Biogeography, v. 31, p. 307–314.

Luoto, M., Kuussaari, M., and Toivonen, T., 2002, Modelling butterfly distribution based on remote sensing data: Journal of Biogeography, v. 29, p. 1027–1037.

Mathieu, R., Seddon, P., and Leiendecker, J., 2006, Predicting the distribution of raptors using remote sensing techniques and Geographic Information Systems—A case study with the Eastern New Zealand falcon (*Falco novaeseelandiae*): New Zealand Journal of Zoology, v. 33, p. 73–84.

Maurer, B.A., 1994, Geographical Population Analysis: Tools for the Analysis of Biodiversity: Oxford, UK, Blackwell Scientific Publications.

McFarland, T.M, C. van Riper III, and G.E. Johnson. 2012, The usefulness of riparian NDVI models in assessing avian abundance and richness: Journal of Arid Environments, v. 77, p. 45–53.

Melesse, A.M., Weng, Q., Thenkabail, P.S., and Senay, G.B., 2007, Remote sensing sensors and applications in environmental resources mapping and modeling: Sensors, v. 7, p. 3209–3241.

Mills, G.S., Dunning Jr., J.B., and Bates, J.M., 1991, The relationship between breeding bird density and vegetation volume: Wilson Bulletin, v. 103, p. 468–479.

Mladdenoff, D.J., Sickley, T.A., Haight, R.C., and Wydeven, A.P., 1995, A regional landscape analysis and prediction of favorable gray wolf habitat in the northern Great Lakes region: Conservation Biology, v. 9, p. 279–294.

Newbold, S., and Eadie, J.M., 2004, Using species-habitat models to target conservation: a case study with breeding mallards: Ecological Applications, v. 14, p. 1384–1393.

Nixon, P.R., Escobar, D.E., and Menges, R.M., 1985, A multiband video system for quick assessment of vegetal condition and discrimination of plant species: Remote Sensing of Environment, v. 17, p. 203–208.

Osborne, P.E., Alonso, J.C., and Bryant, R.G., 2001, Modelling landscape-scale habitat use using GIS and remote sensing: a case study with great bustards: Journal of Applied Ecology, v. 38, p. 458–471.

Palmeirim, J.M., 1988, Automatic mapping of avian species habitat using satellite imagery: Oikos, v. 52, p. 59–68.

Paxton, K.L., van Riper III, C., Theimer, T.C., and Paxton, E.H., 2007, Spatial and temporal migration patterns of Wilson's Warbler (*Wilsonia pusilla*) in the Southwest as revealed by stable isotopes: The Auk, v. 124, p. 162–175.

Prasad, V.K., Badarinath, K.V.S., and Eaturu, A., 2008, Effect of precipitation, temperature, and topographic parameters on evergreen vegetation greenery in the Western Ghats, India: International Journal of Climatology, v. 28, p. 1807–1819.

Rea, A.M., 1983, Once a river: bird life and habitat changes on the middle Gila: University of Arizona Press, Tucson, Ariz.

Robbins, C.S., 1981, Effect of time of day on bird activity: Studies in Avian Biology, v. 6, p. 275–286.

Robinson, T.W., 1965, Introduction, spread and areal extent of saltcedar (*Tamarix*) in the western states: U.S. Geological Survey Professional Paper 491-A: United States Government Printing Office, Washington, D.C.

Sedgwick, J.A., 2000, Willow Flycatcher (*Empidonax traillii*), *in* Poole, A., ed., The Birds of North America Online: Cornell Lab of Ornithology, Ithaca, N.Y., accessed October 17, 2012, *http://bna.birds.cornell.edu/bna/species/533*.

Seto, K.C., Fleishman, E., Fay, J.P., and Betrus, C.J., 2004, Linking spatial patterns of bird and butterfly species richness with Landsat TM derived NDVI: International Journal of Remote Sensing, v. 25, p. 4309–4324.

Shafroth, P.B., Stromberg, J.C., and Patten, D.T., 2002, Riparian vegetation response to altered disturbance and stress regimes: Ecological Applications, v. 12, p. 107–123.

Shafroth, P.B., Cleverly, J.R., Dudley, T.L., Taylor, J.P., Van Riper, C., Weeks, E.P., and Stuart, J.N., 2005, Control of *Tamarix* in the western United States—Implications for water salvage, wildlife use, and riparian restoration: Environmental Management, v. 35, p. 231–246.

Skagen, S.K., Melcher, C.P., Howe, W.H., and Knopf, F.L., 1998, Comparative use of riparian corridors and oases by migrating birds in southeast Arizona: Conservation Biology, v. 12, p. 896–909.

Sogge, M.K., Sferra, S.J., and Paxton, E.H., 2008, *Tamarix* as habitat for birds: implications for riparian restoration in the southwestern United States: Restoration Ecology, v. 16, p. 146–154.

Stromberg, J.C., Beauchamp, V.B., Dixon, M.D., Lite, S.J., and Paradzick, C., 2007, Importance of low-flow and high-flow characteristics to restoration of riparian vegetation along rivers in arid south-western United States: Freshwater Biology, v. 52, p. 651–679.

Strong, T.R., and Bock, C.E., 1990, Bird species distribution in riparian habitats in southeastern Arizona: The Condor, v. 92, p. 866–885.

Tucker, C.J., 1979, Red and photographic infrared linear combinations for monitoring vegetation: Remote Sensing of Environment, v. 8, p. 127–150.

Tucker, C.J., Vanpraet, C.L., Sharman, M.J., and van Ittersum, G., 1985, Satellite remote sensing of total herbaceous biomass production in the Sengalese Sahel—1980–1984: Remote Sensing of Environment, v. 17, p. 233–249.

Tucker, K., Rushton, S.P., Sanderson, R.A., Martin, E.B., and Blaiklock, J., 1997, Modelling bird distributions—a combined GIS and Bayesian rule-based approach: Landscape Ecology, v. 12, p. 77–93.

van Riper, III., C., Paxton, K.L., O'Brien, C., Shafroth, P.B., and McGrath, L.J., 2008, Rethinking avian response to *Tamarix* on the Lower Colorado River—A threshold hypothesis: Restoration Ecology, v. 16, p. 155–167.

Wiens, J.A., and Rotenberry, J.T., 1985, Response of breeding passerine birds to rangeland alteration in a North American shrubsteppe locality: The Journal of Applied Ecology, v. 22, p. 655–668.

Yard, H.K., van Riper III, C., Brown, B.T., and Kearsley, M.J., 2004, Diets of insectivorous birds along the Colorado River in Grand Canyon, Arizona: The Condor, v. 106, p. 106–115.

Yong, W., and Finch, D.M., 2002, Stopover ecology of landbirds migrating along the middle Rio Grande in spring and fall: Department of Agriculture General Technical Report RMRS-GTR-99, Forest Service, Rocky Mountain Research Station, Ogden, Utah.

Appendix A: Extension of Riparian Normalized Difference Vegetation Index NDVI Models to Avian Abundance and Richness

Introduction

Understanding community structure and function is important for the conservation of rare habitats and the species that depend on them (Kantrud and Stewart, 1984; Wiens and Rotenberry, 1985; Debinski and Brussard, 1994; Colwell and Dodd, 1995). In particular, understanding the relationship between habitat distribution and habitat use is imperative to the implementation of successful management actions. A key first step in understanding habitat use is to identify the availability of habitats and the species that occupy them. However, in avian ecology, monitoring birds by traditional on-the-ground field methods can be difficult and expensive because of logistics and time requirements. Since 1972, when remotely sensed imagery became widely available to the public, biologists have been investigating the use of satellite imagery models to identify, characterize, monitor, and predict habitats over much broader landscapes. Gottschalk and others (2005) summarized 109 remote-sensing studies of avian habitat conducted since 1974 (see also Gibson and others, 2004; Newbold and Eadie, 2004; Mathieu and others, 2006), but most of these satellite imagery habitat models focus on single species (Gottschalk and others, 2005). The applicability of remote-sensing models to understanding broader community structure and function remains largely untested, even though avian abundance and avian species richness are important to manage avian communities, especially in habitats that are threatened or rare.

Avian abundance and species richness have been shown to correlate to the remotely sensed Normalized Difference Vegetation Index (NDVI; Jordan, 1969; Nixon and others, 1985; Tucker and others, 1985) in two studies (Maurer, 1994; Lee and others, 2004), but these relationships have not been investigated further. In 1999, the Arizona Game and Fish Department developed a model to predict breeding sites of the endangered southwestern Willow Flycatcher in riparian areas in Arizona (Hatten and Paradzick, 2003; Dockens and others, 2004; Hatten and Sogge, 2007). This SWWF model separates the riparian vegetation into five probability classes based on NDVI and floodplain size (Hatten and Paradzick, 2003). The southwestern riparian woodlands that SWWF rely on constitute a small percentage of the landscape yet support a high diversity and high density of avian species (Knopf and others, 1988). The southwestern riparian woodlands systems are crucial to many species as migratory stopover sites (Skagen and others, 1998; Yong and Finch, 2002; DeLong and others, 2005; Webb and others, 2007) and as breeding habitat (Strong and Bock, 1990; DeSante and George, 1994). However, riparian areas have been degraded because of stresses from agriculture, overgrazing, altered hydrologic regimes, and invasive species (Robinson, 1965; Knopf and others, 1988; Cleverly and others, 1997; Shafroth and others, 2002, 2005; Stromberg and others, 2007; Sogge and others, 2008; van Riper and others, 2008). Damage to these riparian systems has been linked to decreases in populations of many avian species, including Bell's vireo (BEVI; *Vireo bellii*), Lucy's warbler (LUWA; *Vermivora luciae*), and Abert's towhee (ABTO; *Pipilo aberti*) (Rea, 1983; Knopf and others, 1988; DeSante and George, 1994), all of which were listed on the Arizona Audubon Watch List (http://az.audubon.org/arizona-watchlist-2007). Because Hatten and Paradzick's (2003) SWWF model is unique in its applicability to narrow riparian systems and has already been applied to drainages throughout Arizona (Dockens and others, 2004), this model is ideal for investigating its applicability to monitoring avian abundance and species richness. Although this model is extremely successful in predicting SWWF habitat relationships, the applicability of this model to other riparian-dependent species is unknown.

We tested the applicability of the SWWF model to predict the diversity and abundance of a broader riparian-dependent avian community. Specifically, we asked whether the relationships between avian communities and their habitat can be assessed using remote sensing based on two models: (1) the SWWF model, which incorporates NDVI and floodplain size, and (2) a simple model that contains only NDVI. The findings of Maurer (1994) and Lee and others (2004) relating NDVI to avian abundance and species richness led us to investigate the use of this single metric in modeling bird communities more generally in the threatened riparian areas of Arizona.

Because both models sample only a limited amount of the variation within the environment, some guilds of birds will likely fit these models better than others. We therefore investigated two predictions. First, because the SWWF model is finely tuned to a single species, we predicted that the abundance of other birds with similar foraging requirements as the SWWF, insectivorous air-salliers, would better fit into the model than would birds that do not have similar foraging requirements (DeGraaf, 1985). Secondly, we predicted that the abundance of birds that nest high in the vegetation would correlate better with NDVI than would that of birds that nest lower in the vegetation or on the ground (Parker, 1987; Earnst and others, 2005). We made this prediction because we believe that the large trees preferred for nesting are more concentrated in areas with high NDVI. The outcomes of this study could benefit the monitoring of avian populations and their habitats, retroactively and in the future, by providing a readily accessible, inexpensive, and useful monitoring tool.

Methods

Study Area

Our study focused on the riparian community of the upper San Pedro River in southeastern Arizona within the boundaries of the San Pedro Riparian National Conservation Area (SPRNCA), managed by the Bureau of Land Management (BLM). An additional 6 mi of river was monitored in 2008 on The Nature Conservancy land at Three Links Farm, approximately 15 mi north of Interstate Highway 10 (I-10; fig. A1).

The Models

We investigated how well the five probability classes (Classes) and the probability value (Probability) relate to the abundance of all birds, avian community species richness, and several defined avian species of concern (LUWA, BEVI, and ABTO; Arizona Audubon Watch List, 2007; http://az.audubon.org/arizona-watchlist-2007). Probability is the continuous variable representing the probability of a SWWF nest being present at each location (0–0.98), while the Classes represent the continuous probability value split into increments of 0.2 (20 percent probability, where Class 1 = 1–20 percent, Class 2 = 21–40 percent, Class 3 = 41–60 percent, Class 4 = 61–80 percent, and Class 5 = 81–98 percent probability). We also investigated how the NDVI value alone, a major component of the SWWF model, relates to our avian metrics.

Bird Census

We monitored birds on the upper San Pedro River from late May through late July during 3 years: 2005, 2006, and 2008. All study sites were located within the SPRNCA. However, in 2008, 42 points were placed in the additional segment of river at Three Links Farm. In 2005, a random start location was selected, and 242 points were placed approximately every 250 m following the river; these same sites were monitored in 2006. In 2008, a new random start point was selected and 265 new points were placed 250 m apart along the river. The locations of the 2005 and 2006 points had no influence over the placement of 2008 points.

We conducted point counts between 10 min after sunrise and 9:00 a.m. Observers quietly approached points, waited approximately 1 min, and then recorded all birds detected for 5 min. For every bird detected, we recorded the species, detection type (aural, visual, or flyover), and distance to the bird (estimated with a range-finder). All points were monitored four times each in 2005 and two times each in 2006 and 2008. After all points were counted once within a season, we began revisiting points so that replicates occurred at evenly spaced intervals throughout the breeding season, and so that the same number occurred in the first and second halves of the season.

Birds detected between the 5-min count periods and birds only detected as flyovers were not included. Our analyses also were limited to only passerines and woodpeckers. Although the SWWF model was designed for a passerine, woodpeckers are very vocal and therefore easily detected. Richness was calculated as the total number of species detected during both count events, although abundance was averaged over the two count events. As previously noted, we defined our species of concern based on the Audubon Watch list (http://az.audubon.org/arizona-watchlist-2007) for the State of Arizona: Bell's vireo, Lucy's warbler, and Abert's towhee. Additionally, we determined which species were our "common species" for analyses by making note of all species for which individuals were detected at 20 points or more in at least 2 years (table A1). To test our two predictions, we classified the common species of birds by their foraging guild (De Graaf, 1985) and nesting guild (table A1; Parker, 1987; Erhlich and others, 1988; Baicich and Harrison, 1997; Earnst and others, 2005).

Remote Sensing

We acquired Landsat™ 30-m resolution imagery for the San Pedro River corresponding to the years and seasons of our point counts. One terrain-corrected scene was obtained for each year during a cloud-free day, approximately in the middle of the field season: June 14, 2005; June 17, 2006; and June 6, 2008. The SWWF model of Hatten and Paradzick (2003) was then run on the imagery and a DEM of the area to generate a floating-point raster for each scene. Points having zero-percent probability were removed from the original model, but we defined these points as "Class 0." A floating point raster also was generated for each scene containing values for NDVI. We determined the value of Probability, probability Class, and NDVI for all point count locations by using the Sample tool in ArcMap 9.2 (ESRI, 2006) and sampling each raster with the GPS locations of the point counts of the corresponding year. Additionally, we used the Focal Statistics tool in ArcMap to create a moving-window neighborhood to produce rasters for each year containing values for the average NDVI values of the pixels within different neighborhoods around each point (0.8, 4.5, and 10.9 ha), replicating coarse imagery. The new neighborhood NDVI values for each year were then sampled with the point count locations of the corresponding year.

Statistical Analyses

To meet conditions of normality, Probability was transformed with an ArcSine square root (+ 1) transformation. Results are given for the transformed value. We examined relationships between species of birds and abundances of birds with (1) the probability Classes defined by the SWWF model, (2) the Probability value at each point, and (3) the NDVI value at the point. We also analyzed the effect of NDVI on bird abundance and species richness when NDVI was averaged over the three different neighborhood sizes.

When examining the abundances of birds, we averaged the total number of birds detected at a point during the 5-min count period over both counts of that point within a given year. However, to obtain the metric for the number of species present, we determined the total number of species detected across both visits of each point. We included in our analyses only bird detections less than or equal to 50 m of the observer because an analysis of detection frequencies by the program DISTANCE (version 5.0, Thomas and others, 2010) showed that the probability of detection decreased to less than 0.2 after 50 m. Moreover, all birds detected at a point needed to be associated with the point itself. We felt a 50-m radius around each point was a reasonable distance within which to make this association.

Although the points in 2005 and 2006 were the same, we used them as separate units due to a new NDVI and Probability value for each year. The NDVI value differed between the 2 years by an average of 0.065 (SD =0.054). Probability also differed by a substantial amount, averaging a difference of 0.085 (SD =0.111), which would change the probability Class at many points.

We performed analyses with all species detected as well as just the common species, both for species richness and bird abundance. We used multi-factor analyses of variance (ANOVAs) for analyses of bird metrics relative to the probability Classes, and general linear models for analyses of bird metrics relative to the Probability value and NDVI. To account for the effects of year, whether due to observer biases or actual differences in birds or vegetation among years, year was a covariate in all of our models. Nominal logistic regression models were used to determine relationships of our three remote-sensing metrics with our species of concern. Effects of year, probability Class, and interaction terms between them were analyzed with Tukey-Kramer Honestly Significant Difference (HSD) tests.

Results

The addition of the rare species did not change the outcomes, indicating that rare species are not driving the bird-habitat relationships in this area. Therefore, all analyses are reported for only the common species.

Bird Abundance and Species Richness

Probability Classes

The number of common birds and common species detected at each point was significantly smaller in "Class 0" than the rest of the Classes (fig. A2). However, no significant differences were determined between Class 1 and Class 2 nor among Classes 2--5 for abundance (R^2=0.3552; Class: $F_{5,721}$=24.5712, p<0.0001; Year: $F_{2,721}$=28.1136, p<0.0001; Class*Year: $F_{10,721}$=2.9889, p=0.0011) and no significant differences among Classes 2–5 nor among Classes 1, 2, 4, and 5 for richness (R^2=0.1927; Class: $F_{5,718}$=12.7072, p<0.0001; Year: $F_{2,718}$=15.7673, p<0.0001; Class*Year: $F_{10,718}$=2.9821, p=0.0011).

Probability

The abundance of birds detected had a significant positive relationship with Probability among years. R^2=0.3205; Prob: $F_{1,733}$=96.6595, p<0.0001; Year: $F_{2,733}$=117.2826, p<0.0001; Prob*Year: $F_{2,733}$=8.2656, p=0.0003). The number of species detected also exhibited a positive relationship with Probability (R^2=0.1656; Prob: $F_{1,730}$=47.0608, p<0.0001; Year: $F_{2,730}$=40.8129, p<0.0001; Prob*Year: $F_{2,730}$=9.9016, p<0.0001).

In the second model, NDVI alone, bird abundance showed a strong positive relationship with NDVI among years ($R^2 = 0.3489$; NDVI: $F_{1,733} = 133.0523$, $p < 0.0001$; Year: $F_{2,733} = 127.9293$, $p < 0.0001$; NDVI*Year: $F_{2,733} = 7.6737$, $p = 0.0005$). Species richness also increased as NDVI increased ($R^2 = 0.1928$; NDVI: $F_{1,730} = 75.3508$, $p < 0.0001$; Year: $F_{2,730} = 44.7924$, $p < 0.0001$; NDVI*Year: $F_{2,730} = 9.0273$, $p = 0.0001$).

When NDVI was averaged over our three defined neighborhood sizes (0.8, 4.5, and 10.9 ha), we still found positive linear relationships with bird abundance and species richness. Bird abundance showed a relationship with NDVI, when NDVI was averaged over a 0.8 ha neighborhood ($R^2 = 0.3875$; NDVI: $F_{1,733} = 185.5483$, $p < 0.0001$; Year: $F_{2,733} = 130.0491$, $p < 0.0001$; NDVI*Year: $F_{2,733} = 9.7100$, $p < 0.0001$). Species richness also showed relationships with NDVI averaged over a 0.8 ha region ($R^2 = 0.2106$; NDVI: $F_{1,730} = 88.7763$, $p < 0.0001$; Year: $F_{2,730} = 43.6070$, $p < 0.0001$; NDVI*Year: $F_{2,730} = 12.2116$, $p < 0.0001$).

When NDVI is averaged across a 4.5 ha neighborhood, abundance again showed a positive relationship ($R^2 = 0.3323$; NDVI: $F_{1,733} = 109.3058$, $p < 0.0001$; Year: $F_{2,733} = 106.8425$, $p < 0.0001$; NDVI*Year: $F_{2,733} = 9.0490$, $p < 0.0001$), and species richness also showed a positive relationship this NDVI value ($R^2 = 0.1654$; NDVI: $F_{1,730} = 43.0030$, $p < 0.0001$; Year: $F_{2,730} = 38.5454$, $p < 0.0001$; NDVI*Year: $F_{2,730} = 12.5702$, $p < 0.0001$).

Even over the largest neighborhood, 10.9 ha, bird abundance still showed a relationship with NDVI ($R^2 = 0.2727$; NDVI: $F_{1,733} = 46.1348$, $p < 0.0001$; Year: $F_{2,733} = 98.1390$, $p < 0.0001$; NDVI*Year: $F_{2,733} = 5.6373$, $p = 0.0037$). Species richness also was still related to NDVI averaged over 10.9 ha neighborhood ($R^2 = 0.1306$; NDVI: $F_{1,730} = 14.2114$, $p = 0.0002$; Year: $F_{2,730} = 37.2231$, $p < 0.0001$; NDVI*Year: $F_{2,730} = 9.8202$, $p < 0.0001$).

Foraging Guild and SWWF Model

The abundance of insectivorous air-salliers did not differ among probability Classes, although the effect of probability Class was found to be significant ($R^2 = 0.0394$; Class: $F_{5,731} = 3.0153$, $p = 0.0106$; Year: $F_{2,731} = 0.0002$). Only Class 0 had significantly fewer birds than Classes 1 and 3 (Tukey-Kramer HSD test). The abundance of omnivorous ground-foragers also did not differ among probability Classes, although the effect of probability Class was moderate ($R^2 = 0.0365$; Class: $F_{5,731} = 2.1214$, $p = 0.0610$; Year: $F_{2,731} = 8.9333$, $p = 0.0001$). Class 5 had significantly fewer birds than Classes 0, 3, and 4 (Tukey-Kramer HSD test).

Nesting Guild and NDVI Model

The abundance of high open-cup nesters increased with NDVI ($R^2 = 0.0616$; NDVI: $F_{1,735} = 39.2098$, $p < 0.0001$; Year: $F_{2,735} = 4.1773$, $p = 0.0157$), but the abundance of ground or low open-cup nesters also showed this relationship, with slightly better fit ($R^2 = 0.3397$; NDVI: $F_{1,733} = 89.8861$, $p < 0.0001$; Year: $F_{2,733} = 140.2486$, $p < 0.0001$; Year*NDVI: $F_{2,733} = 6.8167$, $p = 0.0012$).

Species of Concern

None of the species of concern had distributions affected by the probability Classes (ABTO: $\chi^2 = 2.122$, $p = 0.832$; BEVI: $\chi^2 = 5.801$, $p = 0.326$; LUWA: $\chi^2 = 4.909$, $p = 0.427$, in nominal logistic regressions after accounting for year and an interaction term between Class and year). However, LUWA were found to show a preference in Probability ($\chi^2 = 5.4628$, $p = 0.0194$; Year: $\chi^2 = 84.9566$, $p < 0.0001$), and both BEVI and LUWA have a marginal preference in NDVI ($\chi^2 = 3.6225$, $p = 0.0570$;

14

Year: $\chi 2 = 30.4271$; and $\chi 2 = 3.5679$, $p = 0.0589$; Year: $\chi 2 = 83.66$, $p < 0.0001$, respectively). ABTO and BEVI were not selecting points with high transformed values of Probability ($\chi 2 = 0.1172$, $p = 0.7321$, and $\chi 2 = 2.9907$, $p = 0.0837$, respectively), and ABTO were not showing a significant preference in points in relation to NDVI ($\chi 2 = 0.5094$, $p = 0.4754$).

Discussion

Understanding the relationships between birds and their habitat is important for the conservation of species and ecosystems, especially those under threat. Remote sensing is a potentially valuable way to define suitable habitat over very large areas with minimal cost and reduced hours of work in the field. Because metrics derived from these remotely sensed data are likely relevant to many species of birds, we investigated the applicability of a species-specific model that had already been developed (that is, Hatten and Paradzick's 2003 SWWF model) for our study sites, as well as a simpler model composed of only one metric, NDVI. We utilized these models to test predictions of general bird abundance, species richness, and specific guilds based on natural history, as well as defined species of concern.

Bird Abundance and Species Richness

Probability Classes

The significant difference found between Class 0, which has zero probability of having a SWWF nest, and the other five classes included in the model, indicates that the SWWF model means of determining whether any chance exists of a SWWF nesting is a useful predictor of whether any other bird species will find that vegetation suitable for breeding. This difference between classes with zero Probability and Probability of greater than 0 is based on a cut-point NDVI value of 0.126 (Hatten and Paradzick, 2003). However, the five classes themselves were not useful in monitoring avian communties.

Probability

Once the probability values were not lumped into classes and were allowed to be a continuous variable, a positive linear correlation existed with bird abundance and species richness. However, all points with a probability of zero were classified as such because of an NDVI value under the cut-point value of 0.126. Therefore, the value saturates and does not account for variation in the range of the low NDVI values. Probability value did have a positive linear relationship with bird abundance and species richness, but this metric worked best for the areas with high NDVI values. When the significance between Class 0 and Classes 1–5 is based on a NDVI cut-point, the data indicate that NDVI might be a better alternative for use in monitoring riparian bird populations.

NDVI and Larger Pixels

NDVI also had a positive linear relationship with both species richness and bird abundance and explained more variation than Probability in both models. Additionally, the positive relationship with bird abundance and species richness was sustained even when the NDVI values were averaged over larger areas, simulating coarser-resolution imagery. As the pixel size became larger, the amount of explained variability (R^2) was reduced, but the relationship still existed. In all of our models, bird abundance had less unexplained variation than richness when modeled by NDVI.

Foraging Guild and SWWF Model

When we limited the birds to those that have a similar foraging strategy as the SWWF, the insectivorous air-salliers foraging guild did not fit into the SWWF model. Air-salliers did not fit the Classes in the model any better than omnivorous ground-foragers, because both guilds showed no relationship with the Classes, indicating that the Hatten and Paradzick (2003) SWWF model may be too species-specific to apply to other birds. However, birds that share some other common natural history trait with the SWWF may be better suited to the model than those that share a different foraging strategy.

Nesting Guild and NDVI

NDVI did not better predict birds that tend to nest high in the canopy structure than those that nest on the ground or in the understory. Instead, birds that nest low were better modeled using NDVI, which may indicate that NDVI increases with the complexity of the understory or the thickness of the low vegetation and is not determined by only a high canopy (Nagler and others, 2004).

Species of Concern

When we examined individual species of concern (BEVI, LUWA, ABTO) and how they fit our models, only LUWA showed a relationship with Probability, whereas ABTO and BEVI showed a relationship with NDVI, indicating that dense vegetation is probably important to these two species. The Classes of the SWWF model were not useful in monitoring populations of our three species of concern.

Although our low number of SWWF detections did not allow for statistical analyses, we believe that the SWWF model is applicable to our study site. The only detections were within the boundaries of Three Links Farm in 2008. Although Three Links farm only encompasses approximately 6 mi of river, this area contained 43 percent of the Class 5 points that we monitored. This area also had the largest continuous sections of Class 5 pixels within our study site. The model seemed to account for the lack of frequent detections of SWWF within the SPRNCA, because it showed that very little prime habitat is available to SWWF in this region, and the habitat that is available is discontinuous.

For monitoring avian communities, NDVI shows promise, having a positive relationship with bird abundance and species richness. However, the linear relationships between NDVI and bird metrics have a large amount of unexplained associated variation. This variability is understandable because NDVI can be affected by many landscape variables, such as the composition of tree species, the way the trees are grouped, the amount of understory, the species composition of the understory, the soil type, and the presence of water (Nicholson and Farrar, 1994; Nagler and others, 2004; Prasad and others, 2008). Additionally, with a 30-m^2 pixel, there is error related to the location of the pixel that determines the NDVI, and to the location of the point count due to the GPS units. With the SWWF model, another source of error is that the model was built around locations of SWWF nests. We related the SWWF model to bird detections, which associated all birds with the point where the observer was standing and not the point where the bird was detected. Despite this variation, strong patterns persisted between NDVI and avian abundance and diversity.

Conclusion

Riparian areas of the desert Southwest, like many ecosystems worldwide, are under threat, leading to declines in many avian species (Rea, 1983; DeSante and George, 1994). Understanding the relationship between breeding birds and their habitat is crucial to avian conservation and management.

Although species-specific models such as the southwestern Willow Flycatcher model have merit in monitoring the individual species for which they were designed, they may not always be the most useful metrics for monitoring all avian species. We found that NDVI, a much simpler metric than the Probability metric the SWWF model creates, is a more reasonable predictor of avian community structure in riparian habitat. Like Probability, NDVI is a continuous variable but Probability disregards low NDVI values, whereas NDVI does not saturate at the low values, providing a much more normally distributed dataset.

We found positive relationships between NDVI and bird abundance and species richness, even when NDVI was averaged over large areas, indicating that even large-resolution imagery can be useful for bird monitoring. Global 250-m^2 resolution MODIS Aqua and Terra satellite data, with a comparable size to our 4.5-hectare neighborhood, is available online. NDVI values can be automatically downloaded with the imagery without the need for image processing, making this data very simple to obtain and work with. Therefore, for the monitoring of species richness and abundance in riparian zones in the Southwestern United States, we conclude that NDVI is a practical means.

If NDVI is to be useful in monitoring birds on smaller scales, further research needs to be conducted to determine what other metrics can be added to NDVI models to strengthen the predictive power. Additionally, by determining which vegetation parameters (for example, canopy structure, understory density, species composition) are the largest determining factors for NDVI, we can better understand which species of birds are more likely to show relationships with NDVI and why.

Further investigations should focus on what other elements can be included along with NDVI to further explain avian community patterns in the riparian areas of the desert Southwest, thereby making NDVI more useful for the management of avian species on a fine scale.

References Cited

Baicich, P.J., and Harrison, C.J.O., 1997, A guide to the nests, eggs, and nestlings of North American birds: Academic Press, London.

Cleverly, J.R., Smith, S.D., Sala, A., and Devitt, D.A., 1997, Invasive capacity of *Tamarix ramosissima* in a Mojave Desert floodplain—The role of drought: Oecologia, v. 111, p. 12–18.

Colwell, M.A. and Dodd, S.L., 1995, Waterbird communities and habitat relationships in coastal pastures of northern California: Conservation Biology, v. 9, p. 827–834.

Debinski, D.M., and Brussard, P.F., 1994, Using biodiversity data to assess species–habitat relationships in Glacier National Park, Montana: Ecological Applications, v. 4, p. 833–843.

De Graaf, R.M., Tilghman, N.G., and Anderson, S.H., 1985, Foraging guilds of North American birds: Environmental Management, v. 9, p. 493–536.

De Long, J.P., Cox, S.W., and Cox, N.S., 2005, A comparison of avian use of high- and low-elevation sites during autumn migration in central New Mexico: Journal of Field Ornithology, v. 76, p. 326–333.

DeSante, D.F., and George, T.L., 1994, Population trends in the landbirds of western North America: Studies in Avian Biology, v. 15, p. 173–190.

Dockens, P.E.T., Paradzick, C.E., and Hatten, J.R., 2004, Application of a southwestern willow flycatcher GIS-based habitat model—an estimate of breeding habitat in Arizona, 2001, *in* Dockens, P.E.T., and Paradzick, C.E., eds., Mapping and monitoring southwestern willow flycatcher breeding habitat in Arizona—A remote sensing approach: Nongame and Endangered Wildlife Program Technical Report 223, Arizona Game and Fish Department, Phoenix, p. 28–59.

Earnst, S.L., Ballard, J.A., and Dobkin, D.S., 2005, Riparian songbird abundance a decade after cattle removal on Hart Mountain and Sheldon National Wildlife Refuges: USDA Forest Service General Technical Report PSW-GTR-191, Washington, D.C.

Ehrlich, P.R., Dobkin, D.S., and Wheye, D., 1988, The birder's handbook—A field guide to the natural history of North American birds: Simon and Schuster, New York.

ESRI, 2006. ArcGIS desktop: Release 9.2. Redlands, CA. Environmental Systems Research Institute.

Gibson, L.A., Wilson, B.A., Cahill, D.M., and Hill, J., 2004, Spatial prediction of rufous bristlebird habitat in a coastal heathland—A GIS-based approach: Journal of Applied Ecology, v. 41, p. 213–223.

Gottschalk, T.K., Huettmann, F., and Ehlers, M., 2005, Thirty years of analysing and modeling avian habitat relationships using satellite imagery data—A review: International Journal of Remote Sensing, v. 26, p. 2631–2656.

Hatten, J.R., and Paradzick, C.E., 2003, A multiscaled model of Southwestern Willow Flycatcher breeding habitat: The Journal of Wildlife Management, v. 67, p. 774–788.

Hatten, J.R., and Sogge, M.K., 2007, Using a remote sensing/GIS model to predict southwestern Willow Flycatcher breeding habitat along the Rio Grande, New Mexico, U.S. Geological Survey Open-File Report 2007–1207, accessed October 17, 2012, at *http://pubs.usgs.gov/of/2007/1207/*.

Jordan, C.F., 1969, Derivation of leaf-area index from quality of light on the forest floor: Ecology, v. 50, p. 663–666.

Kantrud, H.A., and Stewart, R.E., 1984, Ecological distribution and crude density of breeding birds on prairie wetlands: The Journal of Wildlife Management, v. 48, p. 426–437.

Knopf, F.L., Johnson, R.R., Rich, T., Samson, F.B., and Szaro, R.C., 1988, Conservation of riparian ecosystems in the United States: Wilson Bulletin, v. 100, p. 272–284.

Lee, P., Ding, T., Hsu, F., and Geng, S., 2004, Breeding bird species richness in Taiwan: distribution on gradients of elevation, primary productivity and urbanization: Journal of Biogeography, v. 31, p. 307–314.

Mathieu, R., Seddon, P., and Leiendecker, J., 2006, Predicting the distribution of raptors using remote sensing techniques and Geographic Information Systems—A case study with the Eastern New Zealand falcon (*Falco novaeseelandiae*): New Zealand Journal of Zoology, v. 33, p. 73–84.

Maurer, B.A., 1994, Geographical population analysis—Tools for the analysis of biodiversity: Oxford, UK, Blackwell Scientific Publications, 144 p.

McFarland, T.M, van Riper, C., III, and Johnson, G.E., 2012, The usefulness of riparian NDVI models in assessing avian abundance and richness: Journal of Arid Environments, v. 77, p. 45–53.

Nagler, P.L., Glenn, E.P., Thompson, T.L., and Huete, A., 2004, Leaf area index and normalized difference vegetation index as predictors of canopy characteristics and light interception by riparian species on the Lower Colorado River: Agricultural and Forest Meteorology, v. 125, p. 1–17.

Newbold, S., and Eadie, J.M., 2004, Using species-habitat models to target conservation: a case study with breeding mallards: Ecological Applications, v. 14, p. 1384–1393.

Nicholson, S.E., and Farrar, T.J., 1994, The influence of soil type on the relationships between NDVI, rainfall, and soil moisture in semiarid Botswanna. I. NDVI response to rainfall: Remote Sensing of the Environment, v. 50, p. 107–120.

Nixon, P.R., Escobar, D.E., and Menges, R.M., 1985, A multiband video system for quick assessment of vegetal condition and discrimination of plant species: Remote Sensing of Environment, v. 17, p. 203–208.

Parker, K., 1987, Avian nesting habits and vegetation structure: The Professional Geographer, v. 39, p. 47–58.

Prasad, V.K., Badarinath, K.V.S., and Eaturu, A., 2008, Effect of precipitation, temperature, and topographic parameters on evergreen vegetation greenery in the Western Ghats, India: International Journal of Climatology, v. 28, p. 1807–1819.

Rea, A.M., 1983, Once a river: bird life and habitat changes on the middle Gila: University of Arizona Press, Tucson, Ariz.

Robinson, T.W., 1965, Introduction, spread and areal extent of saltcedar (*Tamarix*) in the western states, U.S. Geological Survey Professional Paper 491-A.

Shafroth, P.B., Stromberg, J.C., and Patten, D.T., 2002, Riparian vegetation response to altered disturbance and stress regimes: Ecological Applications, v. 12, p. 107–123.

Shafroth, P.B., Cleverly, J.R., Dudley, T.L., Taylor, J.P., Van Riper, C., Weeks, E.P., and Stuart, J.N., 2005, Control of *Tamarix* in the western United States: Implications for water salvage, wildlife use, and riparian restoration: Environmental Management, v. 35, p. 231–246.

Skagen, S.K., Melcher, C.P., Howe, W.H., and Knopf, F.L., 1998, Comparative use of riparian corridors and oases by migrating birds in southeast Arizona: Conservation Biology, v. 12, p. 896–909.

Sogge, M.K., Sferra, S.J., and Paxton, E.H., 2008, *Tamarix* as habitat for birds—Implications for riparian restoration in the southwestern United States: Restoration Ecology, v. 16, p. 146–154.

Stromberg, J.C., Beauchamp, V.B., Dixon, M.D., Lite, S.J., and Paradzick, C., 2007, Importance of low-flow and high-flow characteristics to restoration of riparian vegetation along rivers in arid south-western United States: Freshwater Biology, v. 52, p. 651–679.

Strong, T.R., and Bock, C.E., 1990, Bird species distribution in riparian habitats in southeastern Arizona: The Condor, v. 92, p. 866–885.

Thomas, L., Buckland, Stephen T., Rexstad, Eric A., Laake, Jeff L., Strindberg, Samantha, Sharon L Hedley, Bishop, Jon R.B., Marques, Tiago A., Burnham, Kenneth P., 2010, Distance software: design and analysis of distance sampling surveys for estimating population size: Journal of Applied Ecology, v. 47, issue 1, p. 5–14, doi: 10.1111/j.1365-2664.2009.01737

Tucker, C.J., Vanpraet, C.L., Sharman, M.J., and van Ittersum, G., 1985, Satellite remote sensing of total herbaceous biomass production in the Sengalese Sahel: 1980–1984: Remote Sensing of Environment, v. 17, p. 233–249.

van Riper, III., C., Paxton, K.L., O'Brien, C., Shafroth, P.B., and McGrath, L.J., 2008, Rethinking avian response to *Tamarix* on the Lower Colorado River: a threshold hypothesis: Restoration Ecology, v. 16, p. 155–167.

Webb, R. H., Leake, S. A., and Turner, R.M., 2007, The ribbon of green: change in riparian vegetation in the southwestern United States: University of Arizona Press, Tucson, Ariz.

Wiens, J.A., and Rotenberry, J.T., 1985, Response of breeding passerine birds to rangeland alteration in a North American shrubsteppe locality: The Journal of Applied Ecology, v. 22, p. 655–668.

Yong, W, and Finch, D.M., 2002, Stopover ecology of landbirds migrating along the middle Rio Grande in spring and fall, Department of Agriculture General Technical Report RMRS-GTR-99, Forest Service, Rocky Mountain Research Station, Ogden, Utah.

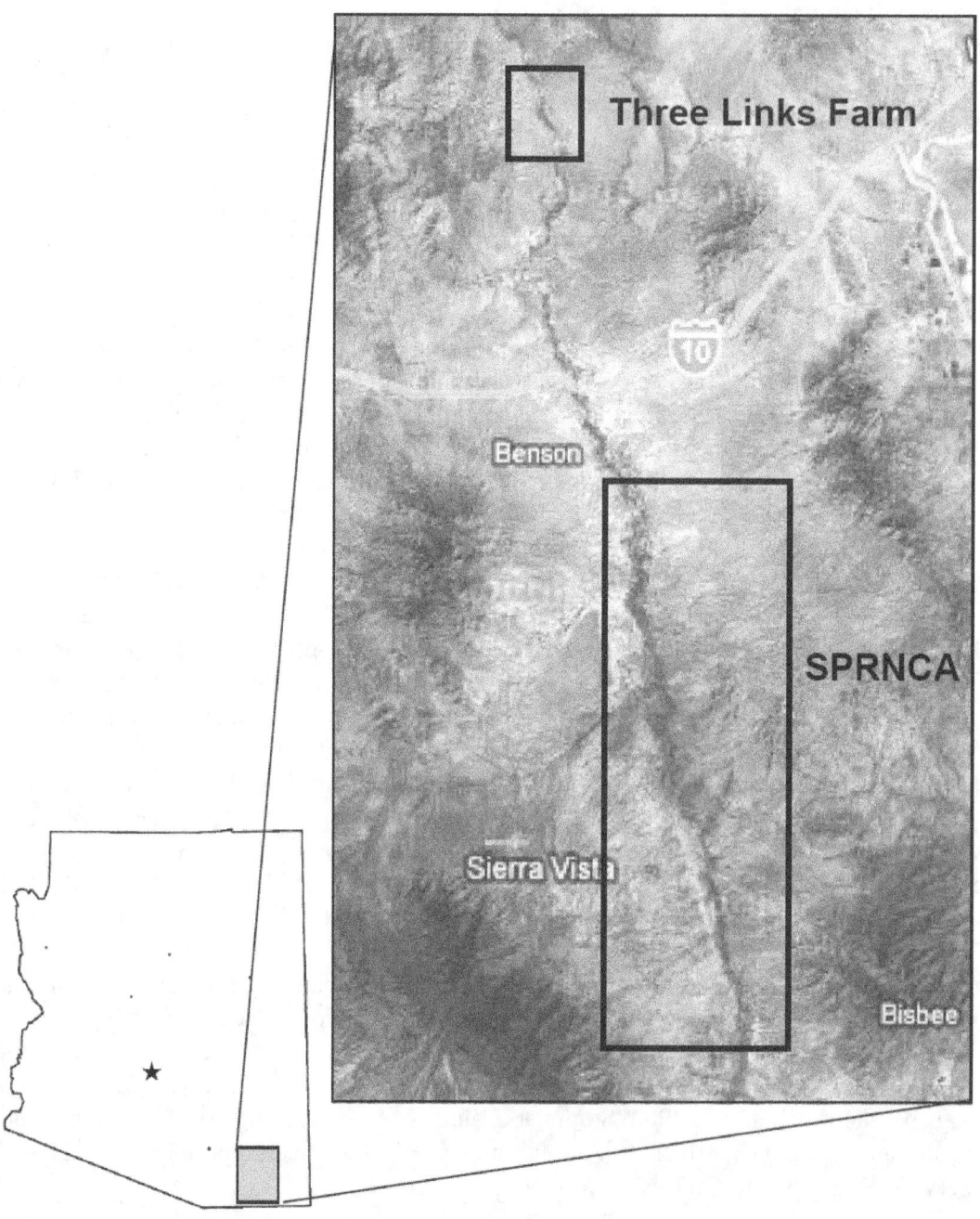

Figure A1. Map showing our study sites along the upper San Pedro River, southeastern Arizona. The San Pedro Riparian National Conservation Area is managed by the Bureau of Land Management, and Three Links Farm is managed by The Nature Conservancy.

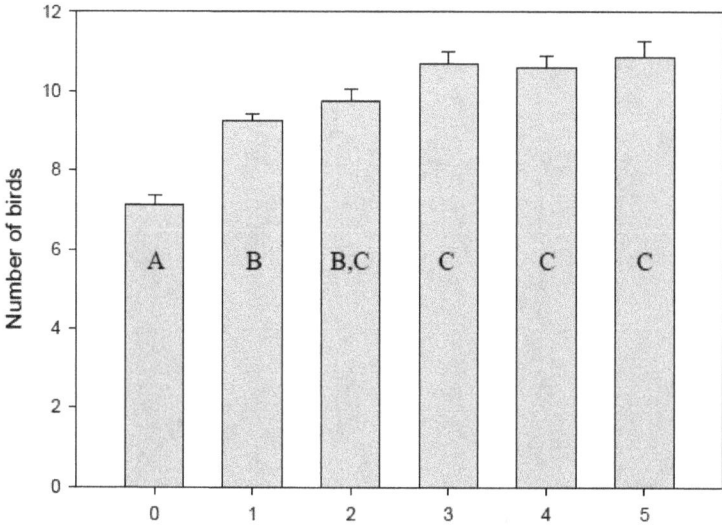

Probability (class) for bird abundance

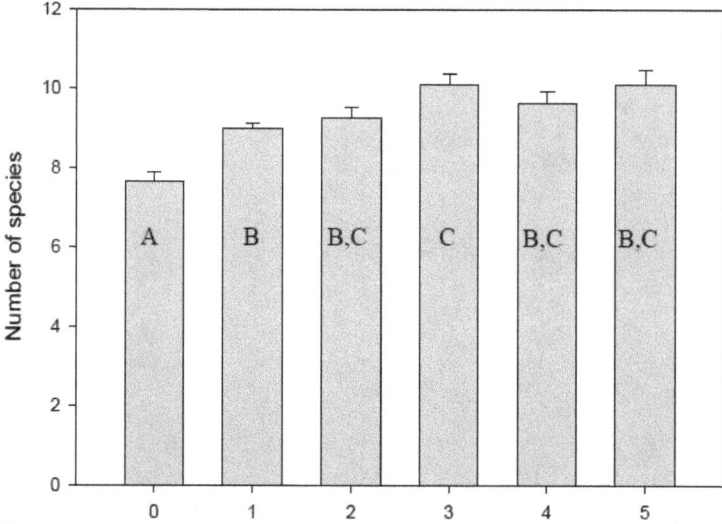

Probability (class) for species richness

Figure A2. Graph showing effects of probability Class on bird abundance and species richness, calculated by Tukey-Kramer HSD tests. Classes not connected by the same letter are significantly different. Classes 1–5 were found to have significantly more birds and more species than Class 0.

Figure A3. Graphs showing regression lines between bird abundance or species richness and probability value or Normalized Difference Vegetation Index (NDVI) for all three years, after accounting for year and an interaction term. NDVI had the strongest relationship with bird abundance.

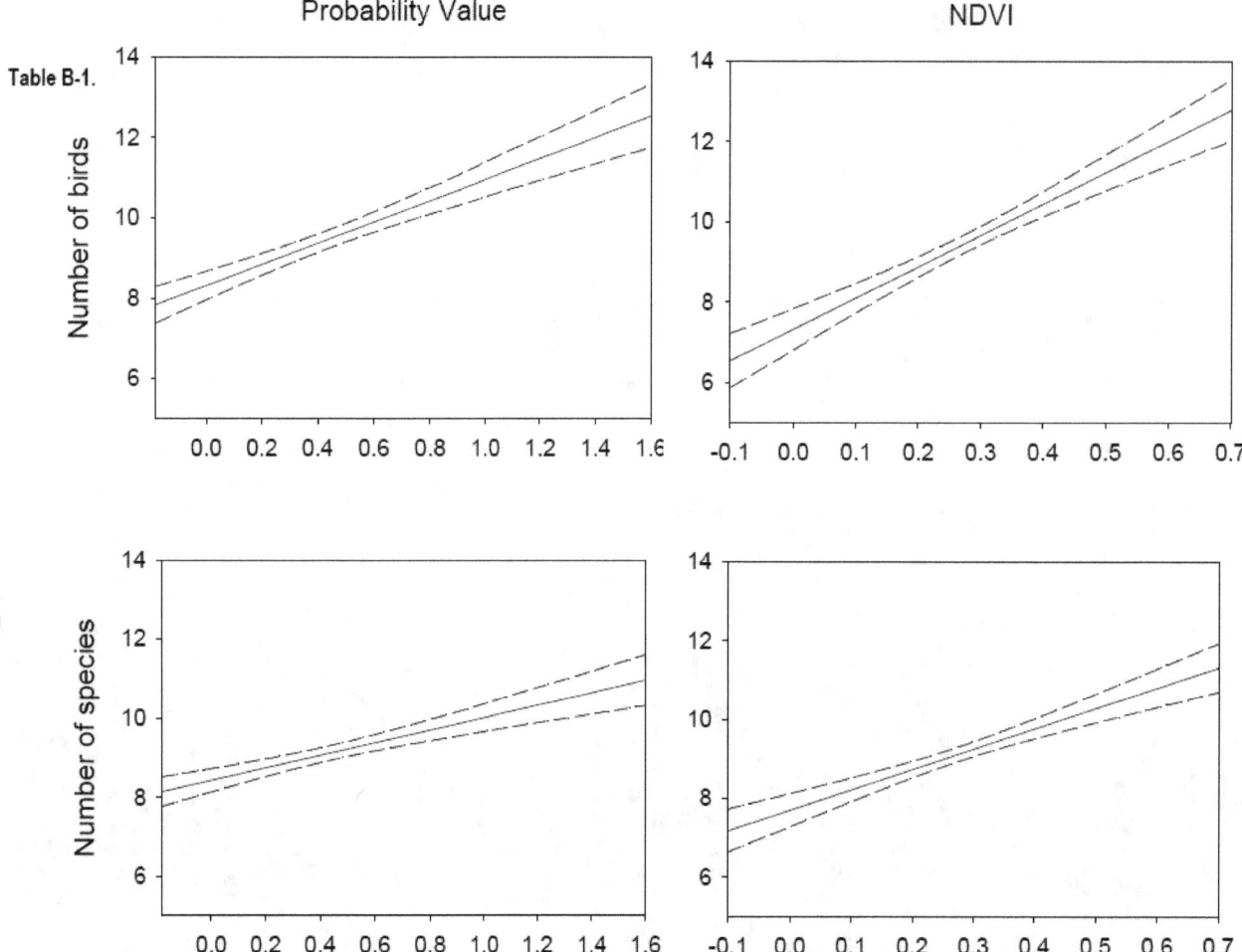

Table B-1.

Table A1. List of common species of birds used in the southwestern willow flycatcher model and birds used in each natural history grouping.

Species	Foraging		Nesting	
	Insectivorous Air-sallier	Omnivorous Ground-forager	High cup	Low cup
Abert's Towhee (*Melozone aberti*)		X	X	
Ash-throated Flycatcher (*Myiarchus cinerascens*)	X			
Brown-crested Flycatcher (*Myiarchus tyrannulus*)	X			
Bell's Vireo (*Vireo bellii*)				X
Bewick's Wren (*Thryomanes bewickii*)				
Botteri's sparrow (*Peucaea botterii*)		X		X
Brown-headed Cowbird (*Molothrus ater*)		X		
Blue Grosbeak (*Passerina caerulea,* formerly *Guiraca caerulea*)		X		X
Black Phoebe (*Sayornis nigricans*)	X			
Bullock's Oriole (*Icterus bullockii*),			X	
Cassin's Kingbird (*Tyrannus vociferans*)	X		X	
Common Yellowthroat (*Geothlypis trichas*)				X
Gila Woodpecker (*Melanerpes uropygialis*)				
House Finch (*Carpodacus mexicanus*)			X	
Ladder-backed Woodpecker (*Picoides scalaris*)				
Lesser Goldfinch (*Carduelis psaltria*)			X	
Lucy's Warbler (*Oreothlypis luciae*)				
Northern Beardless Tyrannulet (*Camptostoma imberbe*)			X*	
Northern Cardinal (*Cardinalis cardinalis*)		X		X
Northern Flicker (*Colaptes auratus*)				
Northern Mockingbird (*Mimus polyglottos*)		X		X
Northern Rough-winged Swallow (*Stelgidopteryx serripennis*)				
Song Sparrow (*Melospiza melodia*)				X
Summer Tanager (*Piranga rubra*)			X	
Vermilion Flycatcher (*Pyrocephalus rubinus*)	X		X	
Western Kingbird (*Tyrannus verticalis*)				
Western Wood Pewee (*Contopus sordidulus*)	X		X	
White-breasted Nuthatch (*Sitta carolinensis*)	X		X	
Yellow-breasted Chat (*Icteria virens*)				X
Yellow Warbler (*Setophaga petechia,* formerly *Dendroica petechia*)				X

*Note that the Northern Beardless Tyrranulet construct globular nests instead of cup nests, but still nest very high in the canopy.

Note: Birds were determined to be common species if they were detected at 20 points or more in each of the 3 years that we conducted censuses.

Appendix B: Comparison of Normalized Difference Vegetation Index NDVI Models for Riparian Avian Abundance and Species Richness

Introduction

Understanding the relationships between birds and their habitat is important to the management and conservation of species and the ecosystems that they depend on (Kantrud and Stewart, 1984; Wiens and Rotenberry, 1985; Debinski and Brussard, 1994; Colwell and Dodd, 1995). In particular, the implementation of successful management actions requires understanding the relationships between habitat distribution and availability, and habitat use. This is especially important in ecosystems that are under threat, such as riparian areas in the southwestern United States. Riparian habitats provide a greater biomass of food and shelter for nesting birds, thereby hosting a much higher diversity of species, than the surrounding deserts (Knopf and others, 1988). These habitats are in danger because of threats from groundwater pumping, cattle ranching, agriculture, and invasive species, such as tamarisk (*Tamarix* spp; Robinson, 1965; Knopf and others, 1988; Cleverly and others, 1997; Shafroth and others 2002, 2005; Stromberg and others, 2007; Sogge and others 2008; van Riper and others, 2008). The destruction of the Southwest riparian areas is reflected by the decline in many species that are dependent on the rivers for one or more parts of their breeding cycle (Rea, 1983; Strong and Bock, 1990; DeSante and George, 1994; Skagen and others, 1998; ; Yong and Finch, 2002; DeLong and others, 2005; Webb and others, 2007). Because avian communities can be used to indicate ecosystem health (Steele and others, 1984; Morrison, 1986; Furness and others, 1993), understanding what habitat parameters best explain avian community structure would allow for more focused management practices along the riparian areas of the desert Southwest.

However, traditional techniques for monitoring birds and their habitat are expensive and often limited in scope. Since the advent of satellite imagery, researchers have been investigating the use of remote-sensing data to identify, characterize, monitor, and predict avian species habitat across large spatial and temporal scales (Palmeirim, 1988; Hatten and Paradzick, 2003; Seto and others, 2004; Gottschalk and others, 2005; Melesse and others, 2007), allowing for the faster and more effective development of management strategies. However, most of these models are designed to monitor a single species (Gottschalk and others, 2005), and the use of remote sensing to understand broader community structure remains largely untested.

In a study to address the use of remote sensing to model general avian community structure (appendix A), we found that avian abundance and species richness correlated with NDVI (Maurer, 1994; Lee and others, 2004), which is sensitive to photosynthetic compounds (Jordan, 1969; Tucker, 1979; Nixon and others, 1985; Tucker and others, 1985), along the upper San Pedro River in southeastern Arizona. High NDVI values correspond to high amounts of photosynthetic activity from thick or green vegetation (Tucker and others, 1985). However, NDVI alone was not determined to be a useful tool for modeling avian communities because a large amount of variation was left unexplained. Therefore, other metrics are necessary to strengthen the relationships of NDVI with bird distributions (McFarland and others, 2012; appendix A).

In order to find additional metrics for modeling avian distributions, we first investigated what vegetation parameters best predict NDVI along the San Pedro River in southeastern Arizona. By definition, NDVI is a measure of vegetation greenness (Jordan, 1969; Tucker, 1979), but we wanted to determine which specific components of the vegetation affect NDVI.

Secondly, we wanted to determine what vegetation parameters best predict avian abundance and species richness. By determining what vegetation parameters are important to birds and how these parameters affect the resulting NDVI value, we can better understand the positive relationship between birds and NDVI.

With the links among birds, vegetation, and NDVI established, we could then determine whether the addition of vegetation parameters to NDVI could increase the predictive power of the model, yielding a better model for use in predicting bird abundance and species richness.

Finally, we wanted to determine whether other metrics derived from satellite imagery could be used to strengthen the power of NDVI to predict bird-community associations and whether this type of model is stronger than those including vegetation parameters. If other remotely sensed metrics can be used in place of vegetation data, on-the-ground vegetation surveys would not have to be as intensive. The only necessary on-the-ground work would be to verify model output.

Methods

Study Area

Our study focused on the riparian community of the upper San Pedro River in southeastern Arizona within the boundaries of the San Pedro Riparian National Conservation Area (SPRNCA), managed by the Bureau of Land Management (BLM); an additional 6 mi of river were monitored on The Nature Conservancy land at Three Links Farm, approximately 15 mi north of Interstate Highway 10 (I-10; fig. B1).

Bird Census Techniques

We monitored birds on the upper San Pedro River from late May through late July 2008. A random start location was selected, and 265 points were placed approximately every 250 m along the river. Points were placed about halfway into the width of the riparian area and therefore differed in distance from the streambed. The point locations were recorded with a GPS unit.

We conducted point counts from 10 min after sunrise until 9:00 a.m. Observers quietly approached points, waited approximately 1 min, and then recorded all birds detected for 5 min. For every bird detected, we recorded the species, detection type (call, song, visual, or flyover), and the distance to the bird estimated with a range-finder. All points were monitored twice during the season. After all points were counted once, we revisited points so that the replicates occurred evenly spaced within different halves of the season.

Birds detected outside of the 5-min count periods were not included, nor were birds detected as flyovers. The analyses also were limited to only passerines and woodpeckers. Additionally, we defined "common species" of birds as those for which individuals were detected at 15 or more points (table B1).

Vegetation Survey

At each point count location, a vegetation survey was carried out within a 30-m^2 area to correspond with the 30-m^2 pixels of the Landsat Thematic Mapper™ imagery. We focused our efforts on four woody tree species: Fremont cottonwood (*Populus fremontii*), Goodding's willow (*Salix gooddingii*), tamarisk (*Tamarix* spp.), and honey mesquite (*Prosopis glandulosa*), although we did make note of other woody species. We used a convex densiometer to measure canopy cover, taking readings 3 m from the point in all four cardinal directions, always facing away from the center. We used the densiometers to gauge the complexity of the understory by estimating total canopy cover and percent canopy cover of each of the four species within two height strata(5–15 m and (higher than 15 m). We also determined the overall canopy cover. Additionally, by counting only the highest vegetation, we estimated what percent of the total canopy cover would be made up of each of our four woody species as if seen from above. To account for the amount of vegetation lower than 5 m that would not be captured in the densiometers (because they lack the ability to accurately gauge canopy cover at low-height strata), we estimated the amount of vegetative cover lower than 5 m in all four cardinal directions approximately 8 m away from the point (an additional 5 m from the densiometer reading locations). Within a 5-m radius of each of these locations, we approximated the percent of the area covered by low woody vegetation. We used an approximate scale, rounding to the nearest 20 percent cover. We also did stem counts of woody vegetation within the 5-m radius, and finally, we noted whether there was water present in the river at each point count location.

We calculated a metric for each of our four tree species representing the total amount at all height strata that would be visible from above, at each of the four locations of each point count:

$$\text{Tree A} = \ (> 5\text{m}) + (\% \text{ open} * \% \text{ cover} \leq 5 \text{ m} * \% \text{ stems}) \qquad [\text{eq. B1}]$$

where,

$> 5\text{m}$ = total percent of plot covered by tree species A as measured by densiometer (> 5 m)
$\%$ open = total percent of plot open to sky as measured by densiometer (> 5 m)
$\%$ cover ≤ 5 m = total percent of plot covered lower than 5 m (visual estimate to nearest 20%)
$\%$ stems = percent stems of tree species A of total number of woody stems

By summing the outputs (eq. A1) for all four woody tree species, we calculated the total cover (Tot Cover) of the plot by trees at all height strata. We then averaged each variable across the four densiometer and stem count sites for each point count location, yielding nine vegetation metrics, including Latitude and elevation (table B2).

Remote Sensing

We acquired one terrain-corrected scene (Path: 35, Row: 38) of Landsat™ 30-m² resolution imagery for the San Pedro River for 6 June 2009, a cloud-free day occurring approximately in the middle of the field season. Using bands from the red and NIR, a floating point raster was generated for the scene containing values for NDVI. We then determined a NDVI value for all point count locations by using the sample tool in ArcMap 9.2 (ESRI, 2006) and sampling each raster with the GPS locations of the point counts. Additionally, we used the Focal Statistics tool in ArcMap to create a moving-window neighborhood to produce rasters containing values for the average (Avg), maximum (Max), minimum (Min), and SD of NDVI values of the pixels within different neighborhoods around each point (0.8, 4.5, and 10.9 ha). The new neighborhood NDVI metrics were then sampled with the point count locations. By averaging NDVI over large areas, we wanted to replicate coarse imagery. These neighborhood metrics also give us a sense of what sort of habitat is available to the birds within larger areas if birds are selecting habitat based on large scales.

Additionally, we acquired a digital elevation model (DEM) of our study site and sampled this raster with the point count locations to obtain the elevation of the points. We used SLOPE and FOCALSUM functions in ArcMap to determine the percentage of a 41-ha neighborhood that was floodplain or flat (Floodplain; slope < 2.5; Hatten and Paradzick, 2003) for each of our point count locations. This yielded 15 remotely sensed metrics per point in addition to NDVI, including Elevation and Latitude (table B3).

Statistical Analyses

We used only bird detections less than or equal to 50 m of the observer for our analyses because an analysis of detection frequencies by the program DISTANCE (version 5.0, Thomas and others, 2010) showed that the probability of detection decreased to less than 0.2 after 50 m. Moreover, all birds detected at a point needed to be associated with the point itself. We believed a 50-m radius around each point was a reasonable distance within which to make this association.

Owing to non-normality, all vegetation metrics except Water and Latitude are log transformed with a $Log_{10}(x+1)$ transformation. Additionally, Floodplain was transformed with an x^2 transformation. We created a matrix of our vegetation parameters and looked for correlations. Similarly, a matrix of our NDVI-related parameters was created and examined for correlations. When two metrics were highly correlated ($r \geq 0.8$), one of the two metrics was removed.

We used stepwise linear regression to determine subsets of the most important parameters to answer each of our questions. Latitude and Elevation were included as parameters in both the regressions using vegetation parameters and those using the NDVI-related parameters (tables B2 and B3), since both can be determined on the ground with a GPS unit or by remote sensing. In the case of adding vegetation parameters to NDVI, if NDVI was not included in the model, we entered NDVI manually and then ran a forward regression. Whenever Water, our only binomial parameter, was included, we used a Student's t-test to determine effect of Water on the response variable.

We performed analyses with all species detected as well as just the common species, both for species richness and bird abundance. However, the addition of the rare species did not affect the relationships found, indicating that the presence of rare species is not driving the bird-habitat relationships in this area. Therefore, all analyses are reported for only the common species.

We compared each step of our regressions using Akaike's Information Criterion (AIC) to test for parsimony and determine the best models of our regressions for modeling avian abundance and species richness. In order to correct for small sample size, we used the corrected AIC:

$$AIC_c = -2 \log \text{likelihood} + 2k + [2\,k\,(k+1)/(n-k-1)], \qquad \text{[eq. B2]}$$

where,

k is number of model parameters and n is sample size (Burnham and Anderson, 1998).

Results

Latitude and Elevation were highly correlated ($r = -0.998$), so Latitude was deleted from regressions using vegetation and those using only remotely sensed metrics (tables B2 and B3). Cottonwood was highly correlated to Tot Cover ($r = 0.8295$), so Cottonwood was removed, leaving nine total vegetation metrics including Elevation (table B2). Many of the remotely sensed metrics derived from NDVI also were correlated, leaving only eight remote-sensing metrics including Elevation (table B3).

Water was included in the stepwise regression models for avian abundance and in the model for NDVI (tables B4 and B5). Willow, Mesquite, and Elevation were included in all four of our regression models for avian abundance and species richness (tables B4 and B5). Additionally, Elevation was included in the model including remote sensing for species richness (table B-6), and Mesquite was included in the model for NDVI (table B4), making Mesquite a part of all models involving vegetation. Total Cover, however, was included only in the model for NDVI and was not a part of models for abundance or richness. Tamarisk was not included in any of our models. Additionally, the only remotely sensed parameters included in our models were Elevation and SD 10.9ha, whereas the other neighborhood covariates and floodplain were not found to be important in explaining abundance nor richness (table B6).

What Vegetation Parameters Predict NDVI?

When NDVI was modeled using our vegetation parameters, vegetation at two height strata (Cover > 15 m, and Cover < 5 m), as well as Total Cover, Water, and Mesquite, were included in the model (R^2 = 0.370; $F_{5, 259}$ = 30.392, p <0.001; table B4). NDVI was found to be 0.063 higher (95% Confidence Interval (CI) between 0.035 and 0.092) at points where water was present (t = 1.969, p < 0.05). However, increasing amounts of mesquite had a negative effect on NDVI (table B4).

What Vegetation Parameters Predict Birds?

Bird abundance was best predicted by Water, Cover >15m, Willow, Mesquite, and Elevation (adjusted R^2 = 0.138, $F_{5,259}$ = 9.445, p < 0.001; table B4). Abundances of birds were significantly high where water was present (1.301, 95% CI between 0.528 and 2.075, t = 1.969, p < 0.05). Increasing Cover greater than15 m and Willow had a positive effect on bird abundance, but increasing Elevation and amounts of Mesquite resulted in fewer birds (table B4).

Species richness was best predicted by Willow, Mesquite, and Elevation (adjusted R^2 = 0.141, $F_{3,261}$ = 15.440, p < 0.001, table B4). Richness increased with increasing amounts of Willow and with Elevation, but richness decreased as Mesquite increased (table B4).

Does the Addition of Vegetation to NDVI Increase Predictability?

When modeled with NDVI alone, bird abundance had a positive relationship with NDVI, but a lot of variation was unaccounted for (adjusted R^2 = 0.098, $F_{1,263}$ = 29.770, p < 0.001). The addition of vegetation parameters to NDVI when modeling bird abundance showed an increase of 5.8 percent in the explained variation, the model included NDVI, Water, Mesquite, Willow, and Elevation (adjusted R^2 = 0.156, $F_{5,259}$ = 10.766, p < 0.001, table B5). Water again raised the bird abundance by approximately 1.080 (95% CI between 0.294 and 1.867). NDVI was the first parameter entered in the regression. Additionally, when compared to how well vegetation predicts bird abundance, NDVI and vegetation together explained only 1.8 percent more variation than vegetation alone (fig. B2).

Species richness also showed a positive relationship with NDVI, but only 2.3 percent of the variation was explained when NDVI was the only parameter included (adjusted R^2 = 0.023, $F_{1,263}$ = 7.182, p = 0.008). However, a stepwise regression with NDVI plus our vegetation parameters did not include NDVI in the model, and the same vegetation parameters were chosen as without NDVI (table B4). When NDVI was manually entered into the model and a forward regression was run, Mesquite, Willow, and Elevation also were entered into the model (adjusted R^2 = 0.146, $F_{4,260}$ = 12.245, p < 0.001; table B5). While this model explained 12.3 percent more variation than NDVI alone, it added only 0.5 percent to the explained variation of the vegetation-only model (fig. B2).

Does the Addition of Other Remotely Sensed Metrics to NDVI Increase Predictability?

The addition of other remotely sensed metrics to NDVI did increase the amount of explained variation for avian abundance and species richness. When the other remotely derived metrics (table B3) were added to NDVI and a stepwise regression was carried out, abundance was best modeled by NDVI and SD 10.9ha (adjusted R^2 = 0.125, $F_{2,262}$ = 19.896, p < 0.001; table B6), where increasing SD 10.9ha increased bird abundance. The inclusion of SD 10.9ha raised the R^2 value only by approximately 2.7 percent from NDVI alone (fig. B2).

Species richness, however, was best modeled with NDVI and the inclusion of only Elevation (adjusted R^2 = 0.102, $F_{2,262}$ = 15.937, p < 0.001; table B6). Again, species richness showed an increase with Elevation. While this model still only accounted for just more than 10 percent of the variation, the inclusion of latitude was better than NDVI alone (fig. B2).

Model Comparison

When comparing the outputs of all of our models for abundance and richness, including those with only vegetation parameters, those with vegetation parameters plus NDVI, and those with NDVI plus other remotely sensed parameters; an AIC analysis revealed that for abundance, NDVI and the inclusion of either vegetation metrics or remotely sensed metrics, were all competitive models ($\Delta i < 2$; table B7). For richness, the vegetation-only model and the last two steps of the model adding vegetation to NDVI were considered competitive (table B8).

Discussion

We found that the vegetation parameters that had the most influence on NDVI generally were not the same parameters that were correlated with our bird metrics, further indicating that NDVI used alone is not suitable for avian community modeling. The only overlapping parameters were Mesquite, which was in all regressions for our bird metrics, and Cover greater than 15 m and Water, which were both selected in a model for abundance.

Certain parameters were incorporated in several models. Mesquite was selected in all models where vegetation parameters were included and consistently had a negative relationship with NDVI and our bird metrics. Because our vegetation surveys encompassed approximately 15 m on each side of the point count, we can assume that areas where mesquite was detected had narrower riparian area than sites without mesquite. Less riparian vegetation would yield a lower NDVI value; these areas would also support lower numbers and a lower diversity of birds.

Willow also was selected in all models for abundance and richness that included vegetation parameters, and always had a positive relationship with our bird metrics. Why Willow was such a strong predictor is unknown, but the influence of Willow on birds was greater than that of Cottonwood. Highly correlated with Tot Cover ($r = 0.83$), the effect of Cottonwood effect was not selected in any models for birds.

Water was included in both models for abundance that incorporated vegetation parameters. The presence of water always increased NDVI as well as our bird metrics. However, the spectral signature of water lowers the NDVI value in mixed pixels (Justice and others, 1985; Pettorelli and others, 2005), so we can assume that the presence of water does not directly increase NDVI but instead allows more vegetation at a site. Areas with water present tend to have full canopies and support more cottonwoods and dense vegetation (Brand and others, 2008), and we would expect these areas also would have more birds (Mills and others, 1991).

Tot Cover was included only in the model for NDVI and was retained in the models, indicating that the composition of the cover, not the amount, is important to birds. Tamarisk, however, was not included in any of our models. Although tamarisk was present at 114 of our 265 point locations, we surveyed only 8 points where 10 percent or more of the cover, as seen from above, was composed of tamarisk. Therefore, the effects of tamarisk possibly could have been lost because of a small sample size. However, willow and mesquite also were only detected in small quantities at our sites—with only 40 points being 10 percent or more covered by willow and 0 points having that much mesquite—yet the effects of these trees still came out in multiple models. Therefore, the effect of tamarisk is inconclusive, but tamarisk does have less influence on birds in our study site than the native shrub species.

Of our remotely sensed metrics, only NDVI, SD 10.9 ha, and Elevation were included in our models. Abundance decreased with Elevation, with more birds occurring to the north, or downstream;

but unlike abundance, richness increased with Elevation, with fewer species present farther north. Since Latitude and Elevation are so highly correlated, either of these metrics could be the basis of this change, but this data indicates that a tradeoff may exist between the number of birds and the diversity an area can support. Additionally, as SD 10.9 ha increased, more birds were present, indicating that more heterogeneous or fragmented areas may support more birds. Floodplain, a metric that was an integral part of Hatten and Paradzick's (2003) SWWF model, was not selected when modeling abundance or richness.

The addition of vegetation parameters to NDVI did increase the predictability of NDVI for abundance and richness, but the increases were small (5.8 and 12.3 percent, respectively). NDVI was the first metric entered when a stepwise regression was run for abundance, showing that NDVI is important in predicting the number of birds present at a site. However, for species richness, NDVI was not selected to be included in the model with vegetation, indicating that NDVI is not as important in modeling species richness as vegetation. We would expect thicker vegetation to yield greater numbers of birds (Mills and others, 1991), but not necessarily greater numbers of species. An increase in vegetative productivity would directly provide more resources to individuals, allowing for higher abundances, but greater species richness would be an indirect product of higher abundances. This could account for why NDVI is more important to avian abundance than species richness.

The results of our model comparisons and our adjusted R^2 values suggest that vegetation is a necessary addition to a model, whether or not NDVI is included. Modeling with NDVI alone explains more variation for avian abundance than species richness, but the addition of other parameters to NDVI dramatically increases the explained variation when modeling richness. Models that include vegetation work best for modeling birds, but the model with remote-sensing metrics was not far behind for avian abundance. Our AIC analyses suggest that, for avian abundance, the model including remotely sensed metrics is just as likely to be the best model as the model including NDVI and vegetation. However, the models including only vegetation parameters to model abundance were not favored by AIC. For species richness, however, the models containing only vegetation and vegetation with NDVI were favored by AIC.

Even with additional metrics included in our models, considerable variation remained unexplained (fig. B2). Much of this variation is probably related to error associated with remote sensing. From the imagery, NDVI is calculated on a 30-m^2 scale, and although this scale is relatively fine for satellite imagery, much variation in vegetation can be missing in a 30-m^2 pixel. Additionally, GPS units often may have associated location error, especially during cloud cover or when underneath tall trees (Wing and others, 2005). However, despite these sources of error and variation, our models included many significant parameters, showing that remotely sensed variables have potential for use in avian community monitoring. Remote sensing can monitor habitat on much larger scales and with less time required than traditional methods, and further investigation of these methods will yield benefits to avian management.

Conclusions

We determined that the addition of vegetation parameters and other remotely sensed parameters to NDVI increased the explanatory power of our models, and that the best models to predict avian abundance include NDVI with either remote sensing or vegetation metrics. The best models to predict species richness included vegetation metrics, with or without NDVI. However, the increases in explained variation are small, and considerable variation still remains unexplained.

Certain patterns were consistent within our models. We can conclude that in general, species richness and abundance increase with higher NDVI and more total cover. The presence of water also resulted in an increase in avian abundance. Our data also demonstrate that more birds and more species exist in areas where riparian habitat has greater width, and in areas with more canopy cover and more cottonwoods. This finding reinforces the importance of conserving and reestablishing mature cottonwood and willow gallery forests along rivers.

Based on the findings of Jones and others (2008), the protection of riparian areas from grazing and development has increased NDVI in these areas. Unprotected riparian areas generally have fewer cottonwoods, less water, and a narrow riparian belt (Jones and others, 2008). Our data demonstrate that areas with high NDVI values, more cottonwoods, more water, and wider riparian zones support high abundances and diversity of avian species, suggesting that the protection of the SPRNCA from grazing since 1988 has increased bird abundance and diversity in the breeding season.

Overall, NDVI models may not be as successful at modeling general avian community structure as they are at modeling individual species (Tucker and others, 1997; Penhollow and Stauffer, 2000; Seoane and others, 2004). Because vegetation structure is so important in modeling avian assemblages, future investigations should examine how particular vegetation parameters can be gathered more easily by remote-sensing techniques, using either vegetation indices or aerial photography. Additionally, the use of purely remote-sensed metrics should be further investigated for species of conservation concern in riparian areas of the desert Southwest, and for the future monitoring and management of at-risk species.

References Cited

Brand, L.A., White, G.C., and Noon, B.R., 2008, Factors influencing species richness and community composition of breeding birds in a desert riparian corridor: The Condor, v. 110, p. 199–210.

Burnham, K.P., and Anderson, D.R., 1998, Model selection and inference—A practical information-theoretic approach: Springer-Verlag, New York.

Cleverly, J.R., Smith, S.D., Sala, A., and Devitt, D.A., 1997, Invasive capacity of *Tamarix ramosissima* in a Mojave Desert floodplain—The role of drought: Oecologia, v. 111, p. 12–18.

Colwell, M.A., and Dodd, S.L., 1995, Waterbird communities and habitat relationships in coastal pastures of northern California: Conservation Biology, v. 9, p. 827–834.

De Long, J.P., Cox, S.W., and Cox, N.S., 2005, A comparison of avian use of high- and low-elevation sites during autumn migration in central New Mexico: Journal of Field Ornithology, v. 76, p. 326–333.

Debinski, D.M., and Brussard, P.F., 1994, Using biodiversity data to assess species-habitat relationships in Glacier National Park, Montana: Ecological Applications, v. 4, p. 833–843.

DeSante, D.F., and George, T.L., 1994, Population trends in the landbirds of western North America: Studies in Avian Biology, v. 15, p. 173–190.

ESRI, 2006. ArcGIS desktop: Release 9.2. Redlands, CA. Environmental Systems Research Institute.

Furness, R.W., Greenwood, J.J.D., and Jarvais, P.J., 1993, Can birds be used to monitor the environment? *in* Furness, R.W., and Greenwood, J.J.D., eds., Birds as monitors of environmental change: Chapman and Hall, London, p. 1–41.

Gottschalk, T.K., Huettmann, F., and Ehlers, M., 2005, Thirty years of analysing and modeling avian habitat relationships using satellite imagery data—A review: International Journal of Remote Sensing, v. 26, p. 2631–2656.

Hatten, J.R., and Paradzick, C.E., 2003, A multiscaled model of Southwestern Willow Flycatcher breeding habitat: The Journal of Wildlife Management, v. 67, p. 774–788.

Jones, K.B., Edmonds, C.E., Slonecker, E.T., Wickham, J.D., Neale, A.C., Wade, T.G., Ritters, K.H., and Kepner, W.G., 2008, Detecting changes in riparian habitat conditions based on pattern change—A case study from the Upper San Pedro River Basin, USA: Ecological Indicators, v. 8, p. 89–99.

Jordan, C.F., 1969, Derivation of leaf-area index from quality of light on the forest floor: Ecology, v. 50, p. 663–666.

Justice, C.O., Townshend, J.R.G., Holben, B.N., and Tucker, C.J., 1985, Analysis of the phenology of global vegetation using meteorological satellite data: International Journal of Remote Sensing, v. 6, p. 1271–1318.

Kantrud, H.A., and Stewart, R.E., 1984, Ecological distribution and crude density of breeding birds on prairie wetlands: The Journal of Wildlife Management, v. 48, p. 426–437.

Knopf, F.L., Johnson, R.R., Rich, T., Samson, F.B., and Szaro, R.C., 1988, Conservation of riparian ecosystems in the United States: Wilson Bulletin, v. 100, p. 272–284.

Lee, P., Ding, T., Hsu, F., and Geng, S., 2004, Breeding bird species richness in Taiwan—Distribution on gradients of elevation, primary productivity and urbanization: Journal of Biogeography, v. 31, p. 307–314.

Maurer, B.A., 1994, Geographical population Analysis—Tools for the analysis of biodiversity: Oxford, UK, Blackwell Scientific Publications.

Melesse, A.M., Weng, Q., Thenkabail, P.S., and Senay, G.B., 2007, Remote sensing sensors and applications in environmental resources mapping and modeling: Sensors, v. 7, p. 3209–3241.

McFarland, T.M, van Riper, C., III, and Johnson, G.E., 2012, The usefulness of riparian NDVI models in assessing avian abundance and richness: Journal of Arid Environments, v. 77, p. 45–53.

Mills, G.S., Dunning, J.B., Jr., and Bates, J.M., 1991, The relationship between breeding bird density and vegetation volume: Wilson Bulletin, v. 103, p. 468–479.

Morrison, M.L., 1986, Birds populations as indicators of environmental change: Current Ornithology, v. 3, p. 429–451.

Nixon, P.R., Escobar, D.E., and Menges, R.M., 1985, A multiband video system for quick assessment of vegetal condition and discrimination of plant species: Remote Sensing of Environment, v. 17, p. 203–208.

Palmeirim, J.M., 1988, Automatic mapping of avian species habitat using satellite imagery: Oikos, v. 52, p. 59–68.

Penhollow, M.E., and Stauffer, F., 2000, Large-scale habitat relationships of neotropical migratory birds in Virginia: The Journal of Wildlife Management, v. 64, p. 362–373.

Pettorelli, N., Vik, J.O., Mysterud, A., Gaillard, J-M., Tucker, C.J., and Stenseth, N.C., 2005, Using the satellite-derived NDVI to assess ecological responses to environmental change: TRENDS in Ecology and Evolution, v. 20, p. 503–510.

Rea, A.M., 1983, Once a river—Bird life and habitat changes on the middle Gila: University of Arizona Press, Tucson, Ariz.

Robinson, T.W., 1965, Introduction, spread and areal extent of saltcedar (*Tamarix*) in the western states, U.S. Geological Survey Professional Paper 491-A: United States Government Printing Office, Washington, D.C.

Seto, K.C., Fleishman, E., Fay, J.P., and Betrus, C.J., 2004, Linking spatial patterns of bird and butterfly species richness with Landsat TM derived NDVI: International Journal of Remote Sensing, v. 25, p. 4309–4324.

Seoane, J., Bustamante, J., and Diaz-Delgado, R., 2004, Are existing vegetation maps adequate to predict bird distributions?: Ecological Modelling, v. 175, p. 137–149.

Shafroth, P.B., Stromberg, J.C., and Patten, D.T., 2002, Riparian vegetation response to altered disturbance and stress regimes: Ecological Applications, v. 12, p. 107–123.

Shafroth, P.B., Cleverly, J.R., Dudley, T.L., Taylor, J.P., Van Riper, C., Weeks, E.P., and Stuart, J.N., 2005, Control of *Tamarix* in the western United States: Implications for water salvage, wildlife use, and riparian restoration: Environmental Management, v. 35, p. 231–246.

Skagen, S.K., Melcher, C.P., Howe, W.H., and Knopf, F.L., 1998, Comparative use of riparian corridors and oases by migrating birds in southeast Arizona: Conservation Biology, v. 12, p. 896–909.

Sogge, M.K., Sferra, S.J., and Paxton, E.H., 2008, *Tamarix* as habitat for birds—Implications for riparian restoration in the southwestern United States: Restoration Ecology, v. 16, p. 146–154.

Steele, B.B., Bayn Jr., R.L., and Grant, C. Val, 1984, Environmental monitoring using populations of birds and small mammals—Analyses of sampling effort: Biological Conservation, v. 30, p. 157–172.

Stromberg, J.C., Beauchamp, V.B., Dixon, M.D., Lite, S.J., and Paradzick, C., 2007, Importance of low-flow and high-flow characteristics to restoration of riparian vegetation along rivers in arid southwestern United States: Freshwater Biology, v. 52, p. 651–679.

Strong, T.R., and Bock, C.E., 1990, Bird species distribution in riparian habitats in southeastern Arizona: The Condor, v. 92, p. 866–885.

Len, Thomas, Buckland, Stephen T., Rexstad, Eric A., Laake, Jeff L., Strindberg, Samantha Hedley, Sharon L., Jon RB Bishop, Marques, Tiago A., Burnham, Kenneth P., 2012, Distance software—design and analysis of distance sampling surveys for estimating population size: Journal of Applied Ecology, v. 47, issue 1, p. 5–14. doi: 10.1111/j.1365-2664.2009.01737

Tucker, C.J., 1979, Red and photographic infrared linear combinations for monitoring vegetation: Remote Sensing of Environment, v. 8, p. 127–150.

Tucker, C.J., Vanpraet, C.L., Sharman, M.J., and van Ittersum, G., 1985, Satellite remote sensing of total herbaceous biomass production in the Sengalese Sahel—1980–1984: Remote Sensing of Environment, v. 17, p. 233–249.

Tucker, K., Rushton, S.P., Sanderson, R.A., Martin, E.B., and Blaiklock, J., 1997, Modelling bird distributions—A combined GIS and Bayesian rule-based approach: Landscape Ecology, v. 12, p. 77–93.

van Riper, III., C., Paxton, K.L., O'Brien, C., Shafroth, P.B., and McGrath, L.J., 2008, Rethinking avian response to *Tamarix* on the Lower Colorado River—A threshold hypothesis: Restoration Ecology, v. 16, p. 155–167.

Webb, R.H., Leake, S.A., and Turner, R.M., 2007, The ribbon of green—Change in riparian vegetation in the southwestern United States: University of Arizona Press, Tucson, Ariz.

Wiens, J.A., and Rotenberry, J.T., 1985, Response of breeding passerine birds to rangeland alteration in a North American shrubsteppe locality: The Journal of Applied Ecology, v. 22, p. 655–668.

Wing, M.G., Eklund, A., and Kellogg, L.D., 2005, Consumer-grade global positioning system (GPS) accuracy and reliability: Journal of Forestry, v. 103, p. 169–173.

Yong, W., and Finch, D.M., 2002, Stopover ecology of landbirds migrating along the middle Rio Grande in spring and fall: Department of Agriculture General Technical Report RMRS-GTR-99, Forest Service, Rocky Mountain Research Station, Ogden, Utah.

Figure B-1.   Map showing our study site along the upper San Pedro River, southeastern Arizona. The San Pedro Riparian National
Conservation Area is managed by the Bureau of Land Management, and Three Links Farm is managed by The Nature Conservancy.

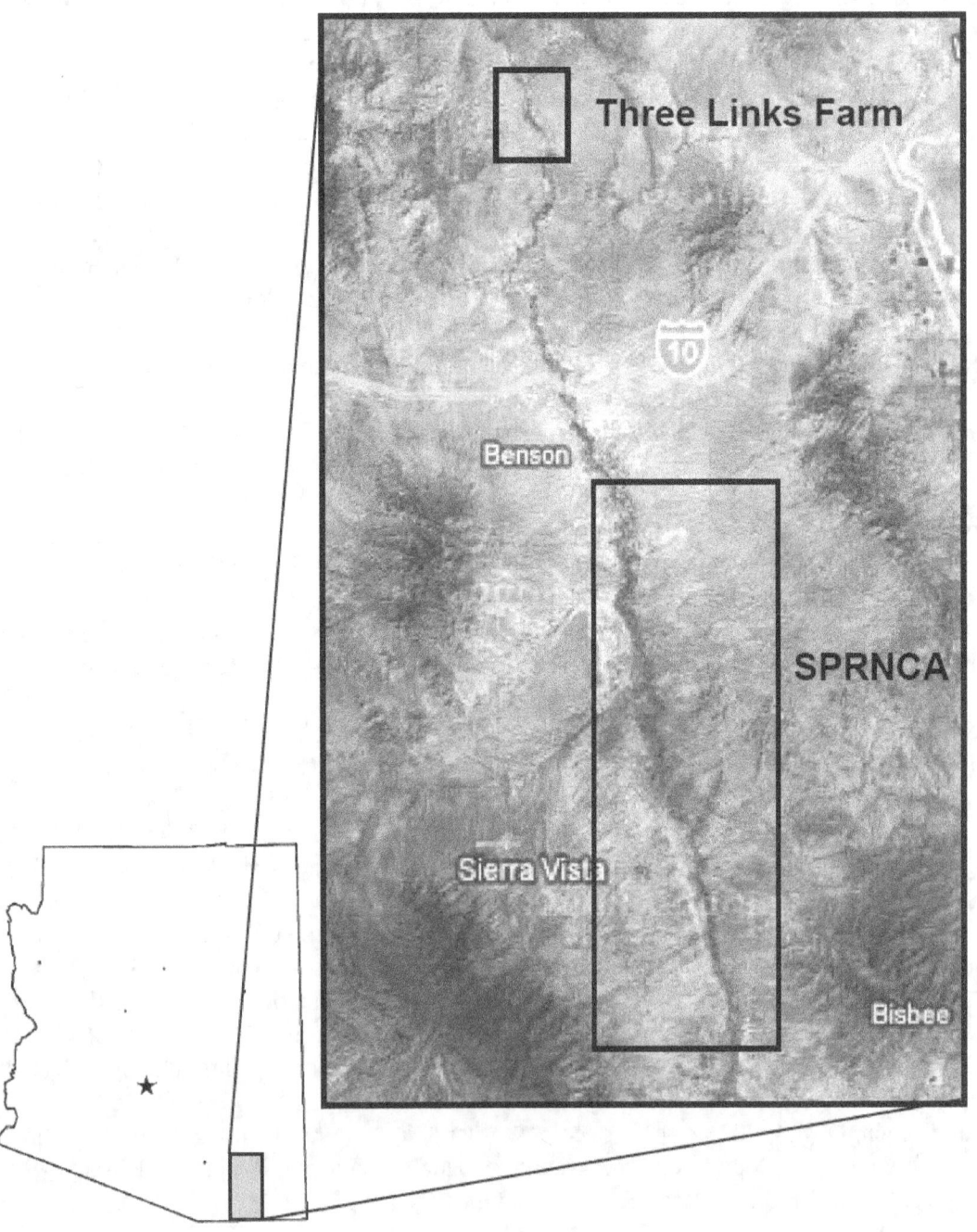

Figure B-2.   Graph showing differences in explained variation (R^2) among models for avian abundance and species richness using Normalized Difference Vegetation Index (NDVI), vegetation, NDVI and vegetation, and NDVI and other remote-sensing (RS) metrics. Richness is best modeled with vegetation alone, while abundance is best modeled with NDVI and vegetation together.

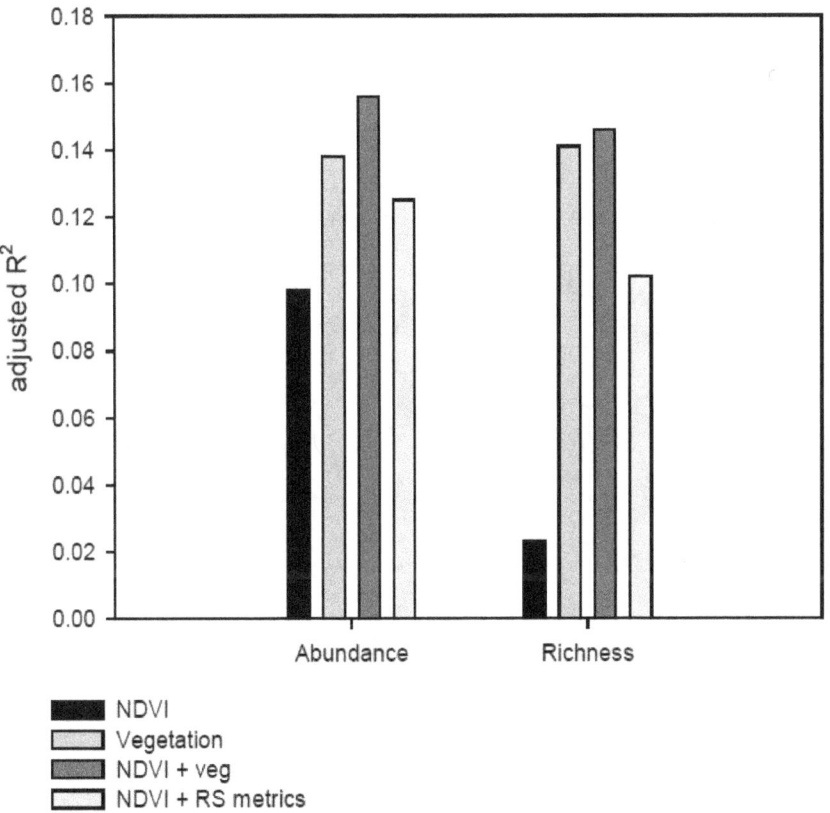

Table B-1. Common species of birds, detected on the San Pedro River from 2005-2008, that were used in our analyses (see Table A-1 for genus and species names). Species were limited to passerines and woodpeckers and required detection at 20 census points or more.

Common Species
• Abert's Towhee
• Ash-throated Flycatcher
• Brown-crested Flycatcher
• Bell's Vireo
• Bewick's Wren
• Botteri's Sparrow
• Brown-headed Cowbird
• Blue Grosbeak
• Black Phoebe
• Bullock's Oriole
• Cassin's Kingbird
• Common Yellowthroat
• Gila Woodpecker
• House Finch
• Ladder-backed Woodpecker
• Lesser Goldfinch
• Lucy's Warbler
• Northern Beardless Tyrannulet
• Northern Cardinal
• Northern Flicker
• Song Sparrow
• Summer Tanager
• Vermilion Flycatcher
• White-breasted Nuthatch
• Western Kingbird
• Western Wood Pewee
• Yellow-breasted Chat
• Yellow Warbler

Table B-2. Final nine vegetation metrics (plus Water and Latitude) used in our regressions for model building. [Cottonwood was left out due to a high correlation with Total Cover. All metrics except for Water and Latitude are $\log_{10}(x + 1)$ transformed to meet conditions of normality]

Parameter	Description		
Water	Presence or absence of water in river at point count location (binomial)		
Tot Cover	Average percentage of total cover (all height strata, as if viewed from above) within four quadrants of point count location; transformed with $\log_{10}(x + 1)$ transformation		
Cover >15 m	Average value (0-5) of low vegetation within four quadrants of point count location; transformed with $\log_{10}(x + 1)$ transformation		
Cover 5-15 m	Average percentage of cover between 5 and 15 m tall within four quadrants of point count location; transformed with $\log_{10}(x + 1)$ transformation		
Cover < 5 m	Average percentage of cover under 5 m tall within four quadrants of point count location; transformed with $\log_{10}(x + 1)$ transformation		
Mesquite	Average percentage of mesquite cover at all height strata as seen from above within four quadrants of point count location; transformed with $\log_{10}(x + 1)$ transformation		
Willow	Average percentage of willow cover at all height strata as seen from above within four quadrants of point count location; transformed with $\log_{10}(x + 1)$ transformation		
Tamarisk	Average percentage of tamarisk cover at all height strata as seen from above within four quadrants of point count location; transformed with $\log_{10}(x + 1)$ transformation		
Elevation	Meters above sea level		
		Correlate	r
Cottonwood	Average percentage of cottonwood cover at all height strata as seen from above within four quadrants of point count location	Tot Cover	0.830
Latitude	Northing value in grid format, NAD27 UTM Zone 12N	Elevation	-0.998

Table B-3. Final seven Normalized Difference Vegetation Index (NDVI)-related remote-sensing metrics (including Latitude) used in our regressions for model building. Some metrics were left out because of high correlation factors with other metrics.

Parameter	Description	Correlate	r
NDVI	NDVI value at point count location (30m2 or 0.09ha)		
SD 0.8ha	Standard deviation (SD) in NDVI values within a 0.8-ha neighborhood		
Avg 10.9ha	Average NDVI value within a 10.9-ha neighborhood		
Max 10.9ha	Maximum NDVI value within a 10.9-ha neighborhood		
Min 10.9ha	Minimum NDVI value within a 10.9-ha neighborhood		
SD 10.9ha	Standard deviation (SD) in NDVI values within a 10.9-ha neighborhood		
Floodplain	% floodplain or flat of 41-ha neighborhood; transformed by X^2 transformation		
Elevation	Meters above sea level		
Avg 0.8ha	Average NDVI value within a 0.8-ha neighborhood	NDVI	0.843
Max 0.8ha	Maximum NDVI value within a 0.8-ha neighborhood	Avg 0.8ha	0.891
Min 0.8ha	Minimum NDVI value within a 0.8-ha neighborhood	Avg 0.8ha	0.844
Avg 4.5ha	Average NDVI value within a 4.5-ha neighborhood	Avg 10.9ha	0.923
Max 4.5ha	Maximum NDVI value within a 4.5-ha neighborhood	Max 10.9ha	0.896
Min 4.5ha	Minimum NDVI value within a 4.5-ha neighborhood	Min 10.9ha	0.797
SD 4.5ha	Standard deviation (SD) in NDVI values within a 4.5-ha neighborhood	SD 10.9ha	0.878
Latitude	Northing value in grid format, NAD27 UTM Zone 12N	Elevation	-0.998

Table B-4. Normalized Difference Vegetation Index (NDVI), abundance, and richness modeled by vegetation metrics. Metrics were selected by stepwise regression analysis. Sample size was 265 for all regressions.

	Term	Estimate	Std Error	t Ratio	Prob>|t|
NDVI	Intercept	-0.036	0.038	-0.950	0.345
	Water	-0.032	0.007	-4.360	<0.001
	Tot Cover	0.058	0.020	2.910	0.004
	Cover > 15m	0.046	0.016	2.920	0.004
	Cover < 5m	0.129	0.025	5.190	<0.001
	Mesquite	-0.110	0.037	-3.020	0.003
Abundance	Intercept	17.450	2.459	7.100	<0.001
	Water	-0.651	0.196	-3.310	0.001
	Cover > 15m	0.697	0.263	2.650	0.009
	Willow	0.955	0.361	2.650	0.009
	Mesquite	-2.670	0.913	-2.920	0.004
	Elevation	-0.006	0.002	-2.810	0.005
Richness	Intercept	0.221	1.833	0.120	0.904
	Willow	0.686	0.286	2.400	0.017
	Mesquite	-2.754	0.740	-3.720	0.000
	Elevation	0.008	0.002	5.470	<0.001

Table B-5. Abundance and richness modeled with Normalized Difference Vegetation Index (NDVI) and the addition of vegetation parameters. When modeling abundance, stepwise regression yielded the parameters shown. NDVI had to be entered manually for richness and stepwise regression followed. Sample size was 265 for both regressions.

	Term	Estimate	Std Error	t Ratio	Prob>|t|
Abundance	Intercept	15.299	2.455	6.230	<0.001
	NDVI	4.877	1.365	3.570	0.000
	Water	-0.540	0.200	-2.700	0.007
	Willow	0.710	0.362	1.960	0.051
	Mesquite	-2.348	0.908	-2.580	0.010
	Elevation	-0.005	0.002	-2.210	0.028
Richness	Intercept	0.111	1.829	0.060	0.952
	NDVI	1.639	1.056	1.550	0.122
	Willow	0.580	0.294	1.980	0.049
	Mesquite	-2.610	0.743	-3.510	0.001
	Elevation	0.008	0.002	5.290	<0.001

Table B-6. Abundance and richness modeled with Normalized Difference Vegetation Index (NDVI) and the addition of other remotely sensed metrics. Metrics were selected by stepwise regression analysis. Sample size was 265 for all regressions.

	Term	Estimate	Std Error	t Ratio	Prob>|t|
Abundance	Intercept	7.466	0.804	9.290	<0.001
	NDVI	5.168	1.404	3.680	0.000
	SD 10.9ha	22.752	7.540	3.020	0.003
Richness	Intercept	0.444	1.853	0.240	0.811
	NDVI	2.525	1.046	2.410	0.017
	Elevation	0.008	0.002	4.910	<0.001

Table B-7.   Akaike's Information Criterion (AIC) comparison of various models for avian abundance. Models with low Δi are more parsimonious, whereas w_i represents the probability of each model being the best, given the data and this candidate set of models. Sample size was 265 for all models.

Model	RSS	p	AIC_c	Δi	$\exp(-1/2\Delta i)$	w_i
NDVI, SD 10.2ha	2040.9	3	-253.530	0.000	1.000	0.201
NDVI, Mesquite, Willow, Water, Elevation	1946.4	6	-253.472	0.057	0.972	0.195
NDVI, Mesquite, Willow	2013.5	4	-253.199	0.330	0.848	0.170
NDVI, Mesquite, Willow, Water	1983.1	5	-253.099	0.431	0.806	0.162
NDVI, Mesquite	2062.3	3	-252.210	1.320	0.517	0.104
NDVI	2111.9	2	-251.303	2.227	0.328	0.066
Water, Willow, Mesquite, Elevation, Cover >15m	1988.4	6	-250.658	2.871	0.238	0.048
Water, Willow, Mesquite, Elevation	2042.3	5	-249.306	4.224	0.121	0.024
Water, Willow, Mesquite	2083.2	4	-248.885	4.644	0.098	0.020
Water, Willow	2154.3	3	-246.834	6.696	0.035	0.007
Water	2220.2	2	-245.295	8.235	0.016	0.003

Table B-8.   Akaike's Information Criterion (AIC) comparison of various models for avian species richness. Models with low Δi are more parsimonious, whereas wi represents the probability of each model being the best descriptor, given the data and this candidate set of models. Sample size was 265 for all models.

Model	RSS	p	AICc	Δi	exp(-1/2Δi)	wi
Elevation, Mesquite, Willow	1322	4	-321.612	0.000	1.000	0.527
NDVI, Elevation, Mesquite, Willow	1309.9	5	-321.438	0.174	0.917	0.483
NDVI, Elevation, Mesquite	1329.6	4	-320.449	1.163	0.559	0.294
Elevation, Mesquite	1351.1	3	-319.265	2.347	0.309	0.163
NDVI, Elevation	1387.8	3	-314.001	7.610	0.022	0.012
Elevation	1418.7	2	-311.851	9.761	0.008	0.004
NDVI	1515.3	2	-299.918	21.694	0.000	0.000

Conversion Factors and Acronyms

mi = miles
ha = hectare
μm = micrometers
m = meters
m^2, meters squared
Δi = index change
SD = standard deviation
$\chi 2$ = Chi Square
MODIS = Moderate Resolution Imaging Spectroradiometer
NDVI = Normalized Difference Vegetation Index